Straightening My Crown

Joani Wangerin

Unless otherwise identified, Scripture taken from *THE MESSAGE*. Copyright © 1993, 1994, 1995, 1996, 2000, 2001, 2002. Used by permission of NavPress Publishing Group.

Scripture quotations taken from The Holy Bible, New International Version® NIV®. Copyright © 1973, 1978, 1984, 2011 by Biblica, Inc.

Used with permission. All rights reserved worldwide.

Scripture quotations are taken from the *Holy Bible*, New Living Translation, Copyright © 1996, 2004, 2015 by Tyndale House Foundation. Used by permission of Tyndale House Publishers, Inc., Carol Stream, Illinois 60188. All rights reserved.

Scripture quotations are from The ESV® Bible (The Holy Bible, English Standard Version®), copyright © 2001 by Crossway, a publishing ministry of Good News Publishers. Used by permission. All rights reserved.

Scripture quotations marked "AMP" are taken from the Amplified® Bible, Copyright © 1954, 1958, 1962, 1964, 1965, 1987 by The Lockman Foundation. Used by permission.

Scripture quotations marked "KJV" are taken from the Holy Bible, King James Version (Public Domain).

Scripture quotations marked "NASB" are taken from the New American Standard Bible®, Copyright © 1960, 1962, 1963, 1968, 1971, 1972, 1973, 1975, 1977, 1995 by The Lockman Foundation. Used by permission.

Scripture quotations marked "NCV" are taken from the New Century Version. Copyright © 2005 by Thomas Nelson, Inc. Used by permission. All rights reserved.

Scripture quotations marked "NKJV" are taken from the New King James Version. Copyright © 1982 by Thomas Nelson, Inc. Used by permission.

ISBN: 979-8-9889937-0-4 (Hardcover), 979-8-9889937-1-1 (Paperback), 979-8-9889937-2-8 (E-Book)

FOREWORD

We have known Joani for decades...

In the late 80s she came to our church and committed her life to Christ. Unlike so many thousands of others who came to Word of Grace to meet God and hear his Word, Joani dove in head first ... and heart first ... into our ministry community. She became a full-time member of our leadership team and rose to a significant place of influence within our church.

Joani's life has been filled with wonder and pain, so the thoughtfulness of this book is rooted in her best and worst experiences with life and God.

This is not just a book of good thoughts and ideas about God. It's a book about life, and we want to encourage you to let Joani's experiences with God transform yours. She will help you move past the impossible questions: Why God? Why me God?

Joani's limitless creativity ... teaching the Word ... developing and discipling leaders ... confronting sin ... leading Christ-centered theatrical productions in the Middle East (yes, really) ... photographing families, weddings, and nature ... communicating prayer requests and updates on behalf of others ... living as a single mom, being very present for her adult daughters and grandchildren ... combined with her huge heart for the Lord ... lives in this book.

Joani writes openly and honestly about how tough life can be and the Lord's tenderness. She will help you keep Jesus with you on the treadmill of your life! The way she does it is a touching tribute to her love for people and her Lord.

As we were writing this for Joani, this scripture came to mind: "The steadfast love of the LORD never ceases; His mercies never come to an end; they are new every morning; great is Your faithfulness." Lamentations 3:22-23 (ESV)

Thank you, Joani, for you. For your relentless love and support of us through years and years of ministry and life.

Dr. Gary and Marilyn Kinnaman

This book is dedicated to…

My father, Jack
who gave me my first picture of what God the Father is like…faithful,
trustworthy, loving, encouraging, counselor, provider, and always ready to lay
down his life for me. Thank you for being
my forever hero, Daddy! I love you!

My sister and brother, Ginny and Chuck
who endured me as their kid sister, championed me as their friend, challenged
me as their peer, and loved me into who I am today. Thank you for your words
of wisdom, unconditional love, and always having my back.

My children, Hannah and Madison
who have been my greatest gifts from God. Thank you for loving me when I
failed you, for caring for me when I needed you, and inspiring me to be a better
mom and example. I love you both more than you will ever know.

My dearest friends,
Amy, Stephanie, Barbara, Tabitha, Michelle, Dani, Val, Lori, Ruth, and Julie.
Thank you for celebrating with me on the highest mountaintops and carrying
me through the darkest of valleys. Forever in my heart.

CONTENTS

A NOTE FROM THE AUTHOR

As I look back over my life, at both the good and bad, I can so clearly see the Lord's hand gently molding me for such a time as this. Every valley and mountaintop intentionally designed to draw me closer to Jesus. Every trial, tribulation, and victory enabled me to realize the potential my Heavenly Father seeded within me as I was knit together in my mother's womb.

Disappointments, loss, rejection, betrayal, sickness… Every hardship intended to destroy me and keep me from the fullness of God's intentions for my life, has in time been used to deepen my love for Jesus and expand my at times wavering faith. As a result, I've experienced a level of love and faith I would not have known had I not walked through the dark places that would ultimately make His light shine most brightly in my life.

It would be here, in my darkest hours, that I would find His most beautiful treasures. Riches I will forever hold close in my heart. It is with this belief, that I have chosen to write this devotional book. It is my hope that as I share my own personal stories, uncover and expose the enemy's lies, that the love and faithfulness of Jesus will be revealed and that God's story will be displayed in mine.

As you continue following God, my prayer is that His unfailing love and truth would prevail over every feeling, or experience, that seems contrary to His promises. It is my hope that my journey to the highest mountaintops and through the deepest of valleys would remind you that, yes! You CAN do all things through Christ Who strengthens you!

May you forever remember that there is NO weapon that can be formed against you that will prosper, for greater is He that is in you than he that is in the world. May you never forget that God's plans for you are to prosper you and not to harm you: plans to strengthen your faith and secure your future. May you have the spiritual eyes to recognize that every seeming failure is actually God giving you a platform to declare His goodness and provision to the world around you.

The truth is, there is no trial or hardship you will ever face that will not fade in the face of eternity. There is no sting, not even death, that can steal, kill, or destroy all the good things God has prepared for you…in this life and beyond. With these things in mind, I want to challenge you. Remember who you are and to Whom you belong. Be strong and courageous, Princess Warrior. Step into your destiny and authority as God's royalty. Daughter of the King, stand up and straighten your crown!

EXPERIENCING THIS BOOK

Since I was a little girl, I have always enjoyed a great story. Even more, I have loved TELLING stories. It started, as it does with most children, with drawing and coloring pictures. I especially remember sketching trees with a swing hanging down from a protruding limb. Of course, a little stick figure of me could always be found sitting on that swing! Swinging under a blue sky with a big round yellow sun, surrounded by green grass and colorful flowers was my childhood personified.

Before I even started school I had graduated from stick people to utilizing my friends to create living pictures. Shows to be exact. These elaborate productions would, with great care, be presented to my family and the surrounding neighborhood boys and girls. Who, by the way, were not only coerced into watching these lengthy presentations, but who were also CHARGED for the experience. I still remember counting my nickels after everyone left. There was always just enough for my favorite treats at the store!

My dad worked for Eastman Kodak, so there were lots of pictures and even movies happening during this time. Waiting for the film to be developed and returned was torment. But when they finally arrived at the local drug store, it was so exciting! You just never knew what you were going to get when you opened that envelope of freshly-developed photos. That's not completely accurate. If the camera had been anywhere near my mom's hands, there was a 99% chance there would be multiple photos with no heads on their subjects. (I'm not kidding! EVERY photo! Ha!)

Movie night, with freshly popped popcorn, was always thrilling. Well, that is until my brother decided to take over the projector, making my recital cartwheels repeatedly go back and forth without landing. (There might have been a bit of screaming and tears during this recurring happening!)

When mobile phones came out with cameras, I was in heaven. I could now capture every "story" as it unfolded around me. Then, just a few years ago I was introduced to the world of professional photography which has only fanned my storytelling gift into flame. Not only have I been able to capture every meaningful moment as it has happened around me, but also God has used photography to open my eyes to the things of His heart.

This is why I decided to include some photos in my book. I'm not going to tell you the story behind each picture, other than to say they were captured during my adventures in Texas, Kansas, New Mexico, Iowa, Missouri, Michigan, Louisiana, California, and France. It is my prayer that Holy Spirit will speak a unique story to you as you look at them and reflect on God's Word.

I've included 40 devotionals. I selected this number because "40 days" in the Bible often referred to a time of challenge that led to spiritual growth.

As you embark on your own 40-day spiritual journey, I encourage you to seek God on His specific purpose(s) for you during this time. Maybe there is a need for repentance in some area of your life, as in the story of the great flood and Noah; or maybe your faith needs to be strengthened as in the story of Ezekiel, Jonah, David and Goliath. Perhaps you're entering a time of testing, trial, and overcoming temptation, as Jesus experienced in the wilderness. Maybe you're questioning God's promises and need direction and clarification for your future, even as the spies were sent to investigate the Israelite's next steps in taking their promised land. Or maybe you need a God-encounter, like Moses had on Mount Sinai or Elijah had on his journey to Mount Horeb. All of these, and more, were 40-day encounters that led to God's destiny for these individuals' lives.

As you begin your 40-day journey, you will see there are five parts to every devotion: A story with scripture; a place for you to journal reflections; a prayer of submission and trust; a commitment to obedience and action; and an invitation to worship and hear God in a way you may not have before. It is this last section, your creative space, that I would like to explain a bit further as well as encourage you not to bypass its potential to impact your intimacy with God.

When we worship God, we can expect Him to be near and ready to speak to our hearts. God has used creation, parables, poetry, prose, artistic imagery, and allegory throughout scripture to speak to His people and reveal truth. Music, clapping, shouting, song, and dance as well as other artistic gifts have all been cited as ways to worship and adore our King.

This last section of each devotion is a place for you to express your love for God. Consider putting on some worship music and maybe have some colored pencils, clay, paints, or craft materials nearby. As you worship, an image, a color, a word, or a scripture may come to mind. When this happens, use your creative space to express what you're seeing, hearing, or feeling. Remember, this is simply an opportunity to worship and hear God's voice in a new way. Incline your ear, knowing God inhabits the praises of His people. Write, draw, color, create….and allow God to reveal His love and confirm His Word to you.

"*And let us consider one another in order to stir up love and good works, not forsaking the assembling of ourselves together, as is the manner of some, but exhorting one another, and so much the more as you see the Day approaching.*"

Hebrews 10:24-25

1 TURNS IN THE ROAD

So often we start a journey thinking we know exactly where the road of life will take us. However, more often than not, it unexpectedly and sometimes unkindly veers us into the great unknown! During those disorienting moments, it's easy to allow fear to rise up within us! (Most assuredly it's an attempt to take us off track and get us out of the will of God.) It is right then, in the midst of the storm, that I continually have to remind myself that I must keep my heart and mind on Christ. I must be saturated in His Word and love! I MUST trust Him.

Times of hurt, betrayal, misunderstanding are all breeding grounds for unholy responses. They are also incredible opportunities to place our trust in God and to grow our faith! That is, if we will only allow that trial to have its full effect in us.

Unfortunately, and too often, I personally forget Who is really in control of my life. I forget Who is with me in the fire and Who is my defender and my only salvation.

It's when I forget these things that I can so easily get into trouble!

As many times as I've found myself in the "fire," I don't know why I continue to allow myself to get distracted and ensnared by the words and actions of others! Why don't I instead, keep my ears inclined and my eyes fixed on my Savior?!

He is faithful! He is good! He is my defender and judge! He is my hope and salvation! Whom shall I fear?

My goodness! This is so simple…and yet so difficult!

Today, I will once again choose to bring my eyes back to The Good Shepherd. I will follow the road He has set before me even when I don't know what's around the corner. The reality is He knows, and that's truly all that matters!

Today I will move forward knowing He will order my each and every step and even forewarn me of the snares that the enemy might set before me! He has promised to guide me with the lamp of His Word into His green peaceful pastures. It is here, in His presence, that I will find the true rest I seek.

Today I will obey His voice, trust in His plan, forgive (even myself) and release those who have wounded me while asking God to help me never hurt them in return.

Too often I have failed miserably at the above, but today I'm repenting (changing the way I think) and giving my thoughts, words, and actions to the Lord. I am trusting Him to display His strength in my weakness, just as He has promised!

Tomorrow is a new day, and I will start again…

Scripture References:

Psalm 119:105 "Your word is a lamp to guide my feet and a light for my path." (NLT)

Psalm 37:23-24 "The Lord directs the steps of the godly. He delights in every detail of their lives. Though they stumble, they will never fall, for the Lord holds them by the hand." (NLT)

2 Corinthians 12:9 "'My grace is sufficient for you, for My power is made perfect in weakness.' Therefore I will boast all the more gladly about my weaknesses, so that Christ's power may rest on me." (NIV)

Psalm 23:1-3 "The LORD is my shepherd; I have all that I need. He lets me rest in green meadows; He leads me beside peaceful streams. He renews my strength. He guides me along the right paths, bringing honor to His name." (NLT)

Reflections:

1) What unexpected turns in my life are causing me to operate in fear?

_____

_____

_____

_____

_____

_____

_____

_____

_____

_____

2) What hurtful words of others am I allowing to distract and/or ensnare me? What lies are keeping me from moving forward?

_____

_____

_____

_____

_____

_____

_____

3) Who do I need to forgive?

_____

_____

_____

_____

_____

_____

Prayer: Take my life Lord, and use every turn in this sometimes frightening road I'm on to bring glory to Your name. Help me keep Your Word hidden in my heart so that it will be the guide for all of my decision-making. May Your truth always direct my thoughts, words, and actions. Help me to forgive myself when I stumble and extend that same grace to those around me. I will look to You in my weaknesses, knowing it is here that You display Your strength. I trust You, Lord, and entrust my future to You! In Jesus Name.

Action Step(s)

_____

_____

_____

_____

_____

_____

CREATIVE WORSHIP

"For I consider that the sufferings of this present time are not worth comparing with the glory that is to be revealed to us."

Romans 8:18

2 A MOMMA'S HEART

I'm missing my girls today! They both live in other states now so I seldom see them. To console myself, I spent the morning serving at church, eating a Crumbl cookie (given to moms after Service), stopping by my mom's gravesite, and looking at old pictures of my daughters.

Motherhood has been the greatest, hardest, and most rewarding role I have ever had the honor to hold!

I can remember before having Hannah (my eldest), I had never even changed a diaper. I was clueless about babies! This is NO exaggeration!

All of my pregnancies were extremely difficult. I was not only incredibly sick with each one, but I also had trouble carrying my babies to full term.

I remember how very excited I was the first time I saw that positive test result. It had taken four LONG years to get pregnant with Hannah and my heart was bursting with a joy I had never known! Then, only six weeks in, I started bleeding and the doctor told me it wasn't a viable pregnancy! I was devastated. I thought all of my dreams of motherhood were coming to an end. Fortunately, the doctor was wrong! But that prognosis filled me with fear...a fear that would follow me for many years.

Hannah was actually born six weeks early and had dangerously high levels of bilirubin. Fear gripped this momma's heart once again! A little over three years later, I had a miscarriage at three months. My little darling's heart just stopped beating. My body refused to acknowledge my baby had died and my uterus continued to grow. It was so traumatic the day I went to the hospital and came home with no baby in my womb. Two years later, at six months, my water broke and I went into premature labor. I delivered my precious son, Daniel, who only lived 1.5 hours. There is no greater pain.

One year later I was pregnant again and touring a show in Turkey when I started having contractions. It was here, in Tarsus (the hometown of the Apostle Paul), that I lost my youngest daughter, Maddie's "hidden twin." Pregnancy was always so difficult for me.

Because of the trauma surrounding carrying my children to full-term, I often had to work through fear: Fear of loss, fear my children would be hurt, fear I would make a mistake, and fear of so many things. Fear can be relentless, and at times it made me completely overprotective, unnecessarily controlling, and I'm sure quite exhausting to those around me.

And though there are still times I may still combat this giant, I more often than not have learned to give those fears to the Lord, whose perfect love casts them far from me.

In this freedom, I have been allowed to see my girls realize their potential. Both are strong women with a passion for justice! They are also extremely gifted with a tenacious grip on excellence.

It has been despite my MANY shortcomings, my gross lack of experience, and my often "not getting it right" that God continues to see my children through this life and its many challenges. Truth be told, I'm still learning how to let them go, how to let them make mistakes without my interference, and how to love and encourage them from afar. More and more I'm trusting the Lord to lead, protect, and empower my girls to victoriously face every giant that may cross their paths! You see, my momma's role has changed. I've graduated from intimate involvement in my children's lives to cheering them on from my knees….with a few hugs and calls sprinkled in!

For those who are single or maybe waiting for a child, I ask the Lord to fill your hearts with courage and an abundance of spiritual children as you wait upon His perfect plan.

Scripture References:

2 Timothy 1:7 "For God did not give us a spirit of timidity *or* cowardice *or* fear, but [He has given us a spirit] of power and of love and of sound judgment *and* personal discipline [abilities that result in a calm, well-balanced mind and self-control]." (Amplified)

Proverbs 3:5-6 "Trust in the Lord with all your heart and lean not on your own understanding; in all your ways submit to Him, and He will make your paths straight." (NIV)

Reflections:

1) Are there any fears related to my children that I need to release to God? (Did my mom make decisions related to me out of fear?)

_____

_____

_____

_____

_____

2) Are there any areas where I need to release control? (Did my mom try to control me, or situations, based on her fears?)

_____

_____

_____

_____

_____

_____

3) Do I need to forgive myself for any mistakes I've made with my children? (Do I need to forgive my mom for the mistakes she made with me?)

_____

_____

_____

_____

_____

Prayer: Lord, I thank you for the blessing of motherhood. Help me to love my children as You love me, and fill my heart and words with Your wisdom, grace, mercy, and loving correction. Keep me from operating in fear and control, but instead let Your love direct my every word and action. Give me eyes to see each of my children as You do and ears to hear their hearts and not merely their words! Give me discernment and Your counsel as I prepare them for life and their call. In Jesus Name.

If you don't have children (natural or spiritual), you will notice I modified your reflections to include experiences with your mom.

Action Step(s)

_____

_____

_____

_____

_____

CREATIVE WORSHIP

"*He will watch over your life; the Lord will watch over your coming and going both now and forevermore.*"

Psalm 121:7-8

3 CHANGE CAN BE SCARY

It is well after midnight, and I cannot get to sleep. It may be because outside my bedroom window, there are about twenty calves bawling for their mommas! It has been going on for hours, and I have little hope of it ending any time soon.

You see, my father is in the process of weaning these calves from their mommas. When calves are between 6 and 9 months old, they are often separated from their mothers in preparation for their next stage in life. Sometimes a nose guard is used for a similar outcome. I know it sounds cruel, but if they are not weaned, it can very quickly create health issues for both the calf and the cow!

In reality, it only takes a few days for both calf and cow to realize they're just fine, and they will stop the bawling. Then they are released back to the same pasture and continue on with life. But until then, it's non-stop moo-ing!

As we are only at the beginning of the process, I'm sure they feel like these few hours of separation are an eternity. (I know that's what it feels like to me right now!! #pleasestopthenoise) So for me, this means instead of "counting sheep" for the next couple of nights, I will be reflecting on cows and enjoying the lack of silence!

Truth is, I can identify with those bawling babies. Though they are fine (and literally JUST on the other side of the fence from their mommas), they don't realize it because things are different. What they have been accustomed to has suddenly changed. Their routine has been disrupted. The familiar is gone, and they are completely outside of their comfort zone! Have you ever been there?!?

Change can be scary!! It's uncomfortable, and it messes with that pesky illusion that we are somehow in control of our circumstances and our lives. (This is so incredibly far from the truth!)

I have to say I can also identify with those momma cows. Having to release not only my children, but also other people I've loved and invested in…ministries I've pioneered and nurtured…visions and dreams I had yet to realize… They have ALL given me cause to cry on more than one occasion. Letting go is never easy!

But through it all, I've come to realize that it sometimes takes embracing the sudden and dramatic changes of this life for God to catapult us into our future, our next assignment, and our destiny! When we let go of the familiar and comfortable, God can expand our trust and empower us to do things we never thought possible! We always have to remember, our God is the God of the impossible. What an exciting prospect that can be when we keep our eyes on

Him!

So tonight, as I'm listening to the non-stop bawling going on outside my bedroom window, I'm reminding myself that change (even when painful) may not always be as bad as it seems at its onset. And though for a "night" I may "bawl" for what was…if I trust and wait upon the Lord…I have every confidence He will work everything together for my good and the good of those He has and will place around me in the days ahead.

Scripture References:

Romans 8:28 "And we know [with great confidence] that God [who is deeply concerned about us] causes all things to work together [as a plan] for good for those who love God, to those who are called according to His plan and purpose." (Amplified)

Joshua 1:9 "Have I not commanded you? Be strong and courageous. Do not be afraid; do not be discouraged, for the Lord your God will be with you wherever you go." (NIV)

Jeremiah 29:11 "'For I know the plans I have for you,' declares the LORD, 'plans to prosper you and not to harm you, plans to give you hope and a future.'" (NIV)

Reflections:

1) What changes in life have created anxiety for me?

_____

_____

_____

_____

_____

_____

2) How do I react to change?

_____

_____

_____

_____

_____

_____

3) What different perspective might I embrace related to changes in my life?

_____

_____

_____

_____

_____

_____

Prayer: Lord, help me to always keep my eyes on You. Help me to trust You will work all things together for my good because the plans You have set before me are to prosper me and not to harm me. I will not be afraid. I will be strong and courageous knowing change gives opportunity to know You better and realize my potential as Your child. I know there is a season for everything, and I choose to trust You in this one. I'm ready to walk into my destiny...with You! In Jesus Name!

Action Step(s)

_____

_____

_____

_____

_____

_____

_____

CREATIVE WORSHIP

"Consider how the wild flowers grow. They do not labor or spin. Yet, I tell you, not even Solomon in all his splendor was dressed like one of these."

Luke 12:27

4 THE CROUCHING LION

I had such a rich encounter with God during worship today! My faith rose to new levels as the lyrics to the songs reminded me of the authority we have been given in Christ Jesus! As we sang, scriptures flooded my mind. We are seated in high places with Christ. (God's amazing love, mercy, and grace on display.) The same Spirit that raised Jesus from the dead dwells within us! We have been given the whole armor of God to help us stand firm against the devil's schemes! We are more than conquerors in Christ Jesus! We can do all things through Christ who gives us strength! Jesus' promise that we would do even greater miracles than He! My worship suddenly turned into prayers of declarations as I spoke life, healing, restoration, and freedom over every individual as the Lord brought them to my mind. It was powerful. It was beautiful. It was life giving!

Then as I've often experienced over the years and just after a victory, satan launched his attack like a crouching lion. It was another of his deceitful attempts to "withdraw" that which had been "deposited."

In the battlefield of my mind, I was no longer seated in high places with Christ but in the dungeons of despair! Thoughts of victory turned to feelings of failure! Instead of a conqueror, I felt conquered! The talons of hopelessness sought to penetrate my soul and the miry clay pulled at me as sinking sand!

How could I be on the highest mountaintop in the morning and then in the shadows of the valley by evening? (I honestly felt like I had fallen into one of David's psalms! I was SO heavy!)

Fortunately, this is not my first rodeo! (Texas laity).

Seriously, I knew I was in a battle! I also knew this battle was going to require the prayers of some faithful friends. With a quick text, I was able to mobilize my closest friends into standing with me in prayer. Every negative thought I was having had to be dispelled. I knew they were all lies, no matter how real and true they felt! (How incredibly crafty is the deceiver!)

Remembering the Scriptures from my morning in worship, I slowly pulled the sword of truth from its sheath. And with the faith-filled prayers of my friends shielding me, and the merciful, loving grace of God, I resisted every lie coming at me…and the enemy fled!

You see, the enemy sought to devour me tonight, but he could NOT! Nor can he you! Remember that!!

Battles will most assuredly come in the days, weeks, and months to come. But when they do, hold FIRMLY to God's promises! They will anchor you in any storm. Additionally, stay closely connected to the body of Christ! There is safety in numbers. Be filled with strength and courage, and KNOW you are not alone!

Scripture References:

2 Corinthians 4:8-9 "We are hard pressed on every side, but not crushed; perplexed, but not in despair; persecuted, but not abandoned; struck down, but not destroyed." (NIV)

Isaiah 41:10 "So do not fear, for I am with you; do not be dismayed, for I am your God. I will strengthen you and help you; I will uphold you with my righteous right hand." (NIV)

Galatians 6:2 "Carry each other's burdens, and in this way you will fulfill the law of Christ." (NIV)

Hebrews 10:24-25 "And let us consider one another in order to stir up love and good works, not forsaking the assembling of ourselves together, as is the manner of some, but exhorting one another, and so much the more as you see the Day approaching." (NKJV)

Romans 8:37 "…in all these things we are more than conquerors through Him who loved us." (NIV)

Reflections:

1) What lies am I allowing to direct my life choices?

_____

_____

_____

_____

_____

_____

_____

_____

2) Who can I call upon when the difficulties of life come at me?

_____

_____

_____

_____

_____

_____

3) What promises in God's Word can I use to replace the enemy's lies?

_____

_____

_____

_____

_____

_____

Prayer: Lord, thank You for Your Word and the power it holds to defeat the enemy who desires to disrupt Your plans for me and my life. Help me to stay strong and courageous when the trials of this life try to discourage and overcome me. Help me to trust in You and Your promise to work everything together for my good. Surround me with those who love You and call You Lord, that together we might overcome and walk in the victory You purchased for us! Help me, Holy Spirit, to remember that I am more than a conqueror in Christ and to stay the course set before me! In Jesus Name.

Action Step(s)

_____

_____

_____

_____

_____

_____

CREATIVE WORSHIP

"*For everything there is a season, and a time for every matter under heaven.*"

Ecclesiastes 3:1

5 SEASONS

I was out by my *dreaming tree* today and the sweet fragrance of wild flowers completely filled the air with the most amazing aroma!

There is nothing like spring. Everything that has lain dormant awakens. New life breaks forth, and the sound of change makes its voice heard.

This is the hope we have as children of God! Just as seasons change in nature, so our lives, situations, and perspectives can also!

What may seem to bring death in one span of time, in another can produce life. What strips us of our hope and identity in one chapter, ignites our faith and secures our value in another. What the enemy intends to destroy in one period, God can actually use to make us stronger in the next!

And though the length of each season may vary year to year (and in some places, may even feel non-existent, thank you Arizona!) the Truth is...nothing in this life ever stays the same! The only exception to this rule is God's incredibly generous and unconditional love - which is the same yesterday, today, and forever.

So as God reminded me today, I want to also remind you. Whatever you're facing, walking through, enduring....do not be dismayed!! Instead be strong and courageous! Remember God's promise to never give you more than you can bear. His promise is to always provide you with a way out, so that you will be able to endure whatever it is you're facing without yielding or being overcome by temptation. Basically, you CAN do this!

It is important to remember there is a season for everything. And when we find ourselves in the 'winters' of life, don't lose sight of the fact that this chapter will pass. It is merely a moment in time...a vanishing vapor in light of eternity.

When we find ourselves in these self-described places of death, we must remember that God is masterful at bringing life from death. He will not neglect the great plans He has established for us. They are bright and filled with hope! Don't let the pruning of one season steal the harvest of joy God has planned for another.

No longer be downcast, but instead stir your faith, lift your eyes, and receive God's unfathomable love and never-ending strength.

Remember God is for you! Do not be afraid. Wait, watch, and see that He is doing a new thing!

I hope this scripture springs forth for you as it did for me when I read it....

"Behold, I will do a new thing; now it shall spring forth; shall ye not know it? I will even make a way in the wilderness, and rivers in the desert." Isaiah 43:19

Expecting, believing, and watching with you!

Scripture References:

I Corinthians 10:13 "No temptation [regardless of its source] has overtaken *or* enticed you that is not common to human experience [nor is any temptation unusual or beyond human resistance]; but God is faithful [to His word—He is compassionate and trustworthy], and He will not let you be tempted beyond your ability [to resist], but along with the temptation He [has in the past and is now and] will [always] provide the way out as well, so that you will be able to endure it [without yielding, and will overcome temptation with joy]." (Amplified)

Psalm 118:6 "The Lord is for me; I will not fear; What can man do to me?" (NAS)

Ecclesiastes 3:1 "There is a time for everything, and a season for every activity under the heavens..." (NIV)

Reflections:

1) In what season am I?

_____

_____

_____

_____

_____

_____

2) What is God showing me during this time in my life?

_____

_____

_____

_____

_____

_____

3) Am I embracing all that God has for me right now?

_____

_____

_____

_____

_____

Prayer: Thank You, Lord, for helping me remember that everything in this life is just a moment in light of eternity. I ask that You would allow me to view every season I walk through as a gift from You. Whether in pruning or harvest, death or life, enable me to see my circumstances from Your perspective and know You are for me and will not give me more than I can handle! Let Your Kingdom come and Your will be done. In Jesus Name.

Action Step(s)

_____

_____

_____

_____

_____

_____

CREATIVE WORSHIP

"*Show me Your ways, Lord, teach me Your paths.*"

Psalm 25:4

6 TEARS IN A BOTTLE

Have you ever just needed to cry, but you simply couldn't?

Sometimes life can be overwhelming!

The loss of a dream, a relationship, the many "unknowns" of what lies ahead, and the fear of failure are but a few of the things that can trigger a sense of hopelessness in our soul. The unfortunate tragedy is disappointments such as these often cause us to shut down, leaving us unable to express, mourn, or release that which intently desires to consume us.

Because we live in a fallen world, we shouldn't be surprised by these less-than-pleasant experiences when they arrive. They are byproducts of the sin and brokenness in the world that now surround us and are sadly unrelenting in their pursuit.

Does this mean we should stay in captivity to our sorrow, pain, and fear? Certainly not! But neither should we deny their existence, consciously or subconsciously. Learning to surrender to God the hidden and hurting corners of our soul allows Him to bring healing and restoration while also deterring the enemy's desire to destroy our health spiritually, physically, and emotionally.

For me, worship is where the battles of this life are won. It is where God not only reveals Himself to me, but also where He visits the deepest recesses of my existence, and He heals both the known and the unknown!

During these intimate times of worship, I sometimes feel tears welling up in my eyes as He reveals His unconditional love for me. Other times, I find myself doing the "ugly cry" with endless tears streaming down my face as He ministers to the deepest parts of my very being. Visiting the places where I know I need Him, He uncovers the surprising caverns where I have unknowingly buried pain and heartache. My soul is laid bare. It is here in the secret places of worship that His healing wings cover me, His living water cleanses and refreshes me, and the Breath of Heaven re-ignites the embers of my heart. Chains are broken and Holy Spirit brings freedom and rest as only He can!

Immersed in God's presence and enveloped in His love, my recent 18-hour drive from Arizona to Texas was such a time as this! Worship music filled my car, as did the Spirit of God. I don't think I've ever experienced anything quite so intense and for such an extended amount of time.

I worshiped and cried. Then, I cried and worshiped. It was beautiful! It was healing! It was exactly what I needed!

I know there were many people covering me with prayer that day. God used those prayers to create a cocoon of healing for me. I will never forget it nor stop thanking God for what He did in my car that day.

If you are feeling overwhelmed by life today, I want you to know, HE CARES! Invite Him into that which is consuming your soul, and let the tears flow. He sees you! He wants to heal you and set you free! And He is ready to catch and store every tear in a bottle, never to be wasted and never to be forgotten.

Scripture References:

Psalm 56:8 "You've kept track of my every toss and turn through the sleepless nights, Each tear entered in Your ledger, each ache written in Your book." (Message)

Psalm 22:3 "But Thou are holy, O Thou that inhabits the praises of Israel." (ASV)

Acts 16:25-26 "About midnight Paul and Silas were praying and singing hymns to God, and the other prisoners were listening to them. Suddenly there was such a violent earthquake that the foundations of the prison were shaken. At once all the prison doors flew open, and everyone's chains came loose." (NIV)

Reflections:

1) What areas of my heart do I need to surrender to God for healing?

_____

_____

_____

_____

_____

_____

_____

2) What is overwhelming me and causing me to shut down?

_____

_____

_____

_____

_____

_____

3) Who can I ask to pray for me while I spend time in worship?

_____

_____

_____

_____

_____

_____

Prayer: Lord, my heart is overwhelmed by all that is happening in my life right now. I need You to invade my circumstances, heal my heart, and set me free from the chains that hold me captive. Show me what's hidden in the deepest parts of my soul and enable me to surrender those things to You without reserve. Help me grieve, help me cry, and help me let go. In Jesus Name.

Action Step(s)

_____

_____

_____

_____

_____

_____

CREATIVE WORSHIP

"My Presence will go with you, and I will give you rest."

Exodus 33:14

7 SAFETY IN COMMUNITY

My time in Arizona was nearing its end. What a blessing it had been to spend time with family and friends!

It had reminded me that when walking through both the good and the not-so-good times, there is nothing like being surrounded by a community of people who will celebrate AND mourn with you!

Though most people don't realize this, I'm a full-blown introvert! I absolutely love people, but unlike extroverts, I'm recharged by alone time and being away from crowds.

Because of this, during the difficult times in life, I have a tendency to isolate. This is not a good idea when facing things that could lead one into the dark places of depression.

As a natural optimist, I rarely deal with depression. However, there have been a few times in my life when particular situations have overwhelmed me to this place of dark isolation.

Living in the country again, I have been reminded how coyotes and even vultures seek weakness and isolation before attacking their prey (not unlike the enemy of our soul). My dad has lost both cows and calves to these strategic beasts of prey. And though this is simply the way of nature, there is a valuable spiritual lesson to be learned in the way these predators wait for the weak and vulnerable to isolate before they consume them.

The enemy and predator of our soul similarly seeks to isolate us during trying times with the intention of devouring who God has created us to be and the call He has placed on our lives.

It's true that it is good to take time away to reflect, contemplate, and self-assess when walking through a difficult season; however, it is equally important to not isolate, but instead stay connected with those who will help you gain perspective. We need people around us who will love and care for us, as well as stand up and advocate on our behalf when necessary! We need those who will pull us up from the miry clay, help us set our feet upon the Rock, and who will both guard and champion our future! We need those who will intervene and protect us from the enemy when we are weak and vulnerable, committing to stay with us until we can once again stand strongly on our own two feet! I am SO grateful to have these kind of people in my life!

It is good to remember that as God's children, we were never intended to do life alone. We were created for fellowship with our Heavenly Father AND one another! It is here in this place of community that true healing, true peace, true joy, and true restoration happens.

So here is a gentle reminder, especially for those of us who are introverts. If you find yourself in the midst of challenging times, don't neglect coming together with the family of God. Don't isolate and don't do it alone! Reach out and let God and His Body walk with you to your place of victory! Together we are ALWAYS better and stronger.

Scripture References:

Ecclesiastes 4:9-10 "Two people are better off than one, for they can help each other succeed. If one person falls, the other can reach out and help. But someone who falls alone is in real trouble." (NLT)

1 Peter 5:8 "Be sober-minded; be watchful. Your adversary the devil prowls around like a roaring lion, seeking someone to devour." (ESV)

Ecclesiastes 4:12 "A person standing alone can be attacked and defeated, but two can stand back-to-back and conquer." (NLT)

Galatians 6:2 "Carry each other's burdens, and in this way you will fulfill the law of Christ." (NIV)

Reflections:

1) In what areas am I isolating and in need of inviting others' help?

_____

_____

_____

_____

_____

_____

_____

_____

_____

2) Why am I trying to do it all on my own?

_____

_____

_____

_____

_____

_____

_____

3) Who can I reach out to and ask to come alongside me?

_____

_____

_____

_____

_____

_____

Prayer: Lord, forgive me for trying to manage my pain and disappointments on my own. Lead me to those who have Your heart and can offer me the encouragement I need right now. Lead me to those who will love me, speak truth to me, and pull me up from this dark place in which I find myself. Give me the courage to be honest and position myself to hear what I need to hear that I might grow and become the overcomer you have created me to be. And as I learn, and become stronger, may I have the opportunity to be there for someone else in his or her time of difficulty. In Jesus Name.

Action Step(s)

_____

_____

_____

_____

_____

CREATIVE WORSHIP

"Finally, brothers and sisters, rejoice! Strive for full restoration, encourage one another, be of one mind, live in peace. And the God of love and peace will be with you."

2 Corinthians 13:11

8 TAKING MY THOUGHTS CAPTIVE

As we travel through this life facing the day-to-day challenges, I OFTEN ask God to help me to take my thoughts captive! (2 Cor. 10:3-5)

For me, taking my thoughts captive means choosing what I will allow to take root in my mind.

I've actually read that on average, we have about 6,000 thoughts going through our minds each and every day! That's a LOT of opportunities for the enemy to get us off track!

Being a natural "storyteller," I've always had to work extra hard in the area of "creative imagination gone wild!" (wink) One thought for me leads quickly to another and to another, and before you know it a full blown story is in place! I've come to realize this is both my strength AND my weakness! It can especially become a problem if I'm walking through a difficult time, and I'm not allowing God's Truth to guide my story's plot!

I remember years ago struggling with a situation between myself and another individual. It was an extremely difficult circumstance and my way of coping with it was to keep replaying the heated conversation between me and this individual over and over again in my head! One day as I was repeating the argument over in my thoughts, I suddenly had this "vision" come into my mind.

I was sitting in front of a TV, and the scenario I was upset about was playing on the screen! As soon as the playback finished, I reached up to push the replay button on the VCR. (Yes, I'm dating myself now! lol) As the video played again, I found myself scrutinizing every word, facial expression and gesture! As the playback came to an end, I reached up and started the video again. This process happened several more times, with me getting more and more upset with each replay.

Then Jesus walked into the room and extended His hand to me! I knew He wanted me to eject the tape and hand it to Him…but I was reluctant! (Don't you hate it when you know the right thing to do, but you just don't want to do it?) I was enjoying watching the footage play over and over again! It was making me feel more and more justified in my offense!

However, Jesus just kept standing there, so I did finally hand Him the tape… reluctantly. (I can be so stubborn sometimes!) When I did, there was this huge release within me. I immediately understood! In halting the repeated replays, I was choosing to let go of my offense. I was choosing to trust Jesus with my heart and the outcome of the situation! I was actually learning to take my thoughts captive!

As I'm sure you've heard before, the greatest battlefield we often face is the war within our minds. So often the stories we repeatedly watch or listen to in our thoughts become rehearsals for unnecessary heartache and tragic outcomes. So now, I do my best to always take my thoughts captive and make them obedient to the truth of Christ, because this is where victory, healing, peace, and joy always await!

Scripture References:

2 Corinthians 10:5 "We demolish arguments and every pretension that sets itself up against the knowledge of God, and we take captive every thought to make it obedient to Christ." (NIV)

Philippians 4:8 "Finally, brothers and sisters, whatever is true, whatever is noble, whatever is right, whatever is pure, whatever is lovely, whatever is admirable—if anything is excellent or praiseworthy—think about such things." (NIV)

Proverbs 4:23 "Above all else, guard your heart, for everything you do flows from it." (NIV)

Romans 12:2 "Do not conform to the pattern of this world, but be transformed by the renewing of your mind, Then you will be able to test and approve what God's will is—His good, pleasing and perfect will." (NIV)

Reflections:

1) What offense am I playing over and over in my mind?

_____

_____

_____

_____

_____

_____

_____

_____

_____

2) What can replace the negative story I am replaying in my mind?

_____

_____

_____

_____

_____

_____

_____

3) Do I need to forgive someone?

_____

_____

_____

_____

_____

_____

Prayer: Lord, You know the struggle I have with the situation that continues to play over and over in my mind. I ask You to give me the courage to push the "eject button" and give my concerns and pain to You. Help me to trust You to be my vindicator and to replace my fears and frustrations with Your truth and Your promises. I will release this situation to You now. I ask You to heal my heart and my mind as I trust You to handle things in whatever way You decide is best. In Jesus Name.

Action Step(s)

_____

_____

_____

_____

_____

_____

CREATIVE WORSHIP

"How beautiful on the mountains are the feet of those who bring good news, who proclaim peace, who bring good tidings, who proclaim salvation, who say to Zion, 'Your God reigns!'"

Isaiah 52:7

Straightening My Crown

9 FIERY TRIALS

Unfortunately, pain and heartache are very real and inevitable parts of this life on earth. We live in a fallen world with broken and hurting people (including us), and as we know, whether intentionally or unintentionally, hurting people hurt people.

Sometimes the pain we experience is rooted in disappointment and the lost hope that we had for someone or some situation to change. When that change doesn't occur how or when we thought it might, we can become discouraged and may even experience some level of depression.

Sometimes there is a feeling of defeat because our prayers seemingly don't produce the results we are hoping to experience. Perhaps the loss of a relationship with a friend, with a child, with a spouse, fill in-the-blank. It's during these times that the depths of despair attempt to consume our soul.

The truth is, there will be times when people let us down. There will equally be times when we let others down, or even ourselves.

False expectations, selfishness, wrong priorities, pride, stubbornness, deception, misunderstanding, and fear are only a few of the things that play into the enemy's path of destruction. The enemy's design is to break what God designed to overcome.

But the Truth is…

Whatever obstacles we face and no matter how insurmountable they may feel, we have the opportunity to pray, trust, and rise up in our faith!

It is crucial during these times of hardship to keep Truth ever before us. God's Word is the perfect light designed by Him to guide our footsteps into the green pastures of His love and provision for our every need.

Kindling our faith with Truth will allow us to walk through the fiery trials of this life with hope and assurance! Because no matter how fierce any "fire" might be, we will always have a pathway to victory in Christ!

When we are faced with trials, the reality is we also are given a choice. Will we allow the fiery trial to consume us? OR instead, will we invite Holy Spirit to use that fire to refine us, heal us, and ignite our faith into a blaze of glory that will display His glory!

We can not only expect the enemy to make attempts at stealing our identity and value during these times, but we must also remember that our value is not in what we deem as a success or failure, but in the victory God has provided us through His Son Jesus Christ.

It is here in the heat of His refining fire, that God exchanges our weaknesses for His strength and His beauty for our ashes. He provides us with a platform to crush the lies of the enemy and ignite faith in others.

So be patient and embrace the trial. God is finishing a work *in* you, so He can work *through* you.

Scripture References:

I Peter 4:12-13 "Dear friends, do not be surprised at the fiery ordeal that has come on you to test you, as though something strange were happening to you. But rejoice inasmuch as you participate in the sufferings of Christ, so that you may be overjoyed when His glory is revealed." (NIV)

I Peter 1:7 "These have come so that the proven genuineness of your faith—of greater worth than gold, which perishes even though refined by fire—may result in praise, glory and honor when Jesus Christ is revealed." (NIV)

Isaiah 61:3 "and provide for those who grieve in Zion— to bestow on them a crown of beauty instead of ashes, the oil of joy instead of mourning, and a garment of praise instead of a spirit of despair..." (NIV)

James 1:2-4 "Consider it pure joy, my brothers and sisters, whenever you face trials of many kinds, because you know that the testing of your faith produces perseverance. Let perseverance finish its work so that you may be mature and complete, not lacking anything." (NIV)

Reflections:

1) In what area am I feeling disappointed and defeated?

_____

_____

_____

_____

_____

2) What lies am I believing?

_____

_____

_____

_____

_____

_____

_____

3) What is the TRUTH about my situation, according to God's Word?

_____

_____

_____

_____

_____

_____

_____

Prayer: Father, today I choose to give You my feelings of disappointment, despair, and defeat. I will not allow this fire to consume me, but instead ask that You use it to refine me for Your Kingdom purposes. Give me eyes to see and ears to hear Your redemptive purpose in everything the enemy has attempted to use against me. I receive Your strength in my weakness and Your beauty for my ashes. Ignite my faith and cause everything intended to destroy me to instead be a platform for You to display your Glory. In Jesus Name.

Action Step(s)

_____

_____

_____

_____

_____

_____

_____

CREATIVE WORSHIP

"He stilled the storm to a whisper; the waves of the sea were hushed."

Psalm 107:29

10 BE FILLED WITH COURAGE

Lately life has felt somewhat surreal.

Loss…yet gain
Sorrow…yet joy
Despair…yet hope
Timidity…yet courage
Weakness…yet strength
Uncertainty…yet trust
Disappointment…yet encouragement
Failure…yet success
Pain…yet comfort
Rejection…yet acceptance
Paralysis…yet growth
Loneliness…yet contentment

I've felt EVERY one of these intensely at some point over the last few weeks. Fortunately, the latter has more often than not overcome the former! As time goes by, more and more, I find myself quickly moving from thoughts of defeat to those of victory.

It has made me realize that the fiery trials of my past have strengthened my faith to a new level! In fact, this season has been like no other.

More and more Truth prevails in my emotions and thoughts. With each passing day, I continue my practice of "taking my thoughts captive," trusting in the goodness of God, and wielding the Sword of the Spirit. I meditate daily on the Truth, remembering that the Word of God is alive and active, sharper than any double-edged sword, and penetrates precisely even to the dividing of soul and spirit, joints and marrow; it judges the thoughts and attitudes of the heart. (Hebrews 4:12)

These words whispered to me during a time of prayer now echo in my heart without ceasing: "Every lie of the enemy intended for our destruction meets its own destruction in the light of God's powerful Word!"

So today I want to encourage you. When the trials of this life seem more than you can take and when the hurtful words, the bad report, and the overwhelming pressures seek to steal your hope, kill your vision, or destroy your future, take courage.

God has gone before you. Not ONE fiery trial will be wasted! For what the enemy has meant for evil, God is turning into your field of favor! The result of your journey, your battle, and your victory is the opportunity for His story to be displayed in yours.

Be filled with courage. Count it all joy! Embrace the difficulty and press onward! All things great are just ahead!

Scripture References:

Hebrews 4:12 "For the word of God is alive and active. Sharper than any double-edged sword, it penetrates even to dividing soul and spirit, joints and marrow; it judges the thoughts and attitudes of the heart." (NIV)

Deuteronomy 31:6 "Be strong and courageous. Do not be afraid or terrified because of them, for the Lord your God goes with you; He will never leave you nor forsake you." (NIV)

2 Chronicles 20:15 "…This is what the Lord says to you: 'Do not be afraid or discouraged because of this vast army. For the battle is not yours, but God's." (NIV)

Deuteronomy 28:13 "The Lord will make you the head, not the tail. If you pay attention to the commands of the Lord your God that I give you this day and carefully follow them, you will always be at the top, never at the bottom." (NIV)

Philippians 4:13 "I can do all this through Him Who gives me strength." (NIV)

Reflections:

1) What thoughts or attitudes in my heart do I need to re-examine?

_____

_____

_____

_____

_____

_____

_____

_____

2) What sword do I need to pull from its sheath to overcome the lies I'm believing?

_____

_____

_____

_____

_____

_____

3) How am I going to 'embrace' the difficulty I'm facing and press onward?

_____

_____

_____

_____

_____

Prayer: Lord, I invite You into my life challenges today. Though I feel overwhelmed, I know I can trust You to walk me through what I'm experiencing in my heart and emotions. Help me to be brave, wise, discerning, and full of Your strength. Guide me in Your Word that I might defeat my enemy with the sword of Your Spirit. I will stand on Your promises, filled with hope, knowing the battle belongs to You! In Jesus Name!

Action Step(s)

_____

_____

_____

_____

_____

_____

CREATIVE WORSHIP

"And let us not grow weary of doing good, for in due season we will reap,
if we do not give up."

Galatians 6:9

11 NO MORE COMPLAINING

Hair clipped up in a knot, raincoat zipped up and seatbelt secured. That was me heading BACK to the grocery store today to pick up the few items I forgot to pick up when I was at the grocery store yesterday! Ugh!

I hate shopping…of any kind really!

I don't like having to put on makeup and fix my hair.

And as much as I love the rain, I much prefer watching it from inside my dry house as opposed to going out into it!

BUT sometimes we have to do things we don't especially enjoy!

After feeling sorry for myself for a few moments. (OK, maybe a bit longer than a moment.) I remembered that today was Good Friday.

The day my Lord was falsely accused and mocked, scourged and beaten, forced to carry the weight of His own cross, endured nails being driven through His hands and feet, and then hung for hours on a wooden cross to pay MY debt.

And I was complaining about what?!

Lord, forgive me when I lose perspective. When I selfishly spend too much time thinking about me, and all that is 'wrong' in my world! Forgive me for not being more grateful and for allowing the inconveniences of daily life to somehow skew what is important and what is not!

I am grateful! I am grateful I have hair to put up in a clip because a few years ago, when I was going through breast cancer treatments, I did not!

I am grateful for the rain that encourages me to wear a cute raincoat and for the refreshing water it provides for the creation You made for my enjoyment.

I am grateful that I have a car, with a safety belt designed to keep me from harm, so that I *can* drive to different places to shop for the necessary things in this life.

Today I'm exchanging my complaining attitude for one of thankfulness! I'm asking the Lord for His perspective in every situation going forward and *not* my limited one!

I am embracing this journey, knowing God's correction is yet another demonstration of His unfathomable love! Are you embracing yours?

Scripture References:

1 Corinthians 10:10 "Nor grumble, as some of them did, and were destroyed by the destroyer." (ESV)

Philippians 2:14 "Do all things without grumbling or disputing…" (ESV)

Job 9:27 "Though I say, 'I will forget my complaint, I will leave off my sad countenance and be cheerful…'" (NASB)

Lamentations 3:39-40 "Why should any living mortal, or any man, Offer complaint in view of his sins? Let us examine and probe our ways, And let us return to the LORD." (NASB)

1 Thessalonians 5:16-18 "Rejoice always, pray continually, give thanks in all circumstances; for this is God's will for you in Christ Jesus." (NIV)

Psalm 118:24 "This is the day that the LORD has made; let us rejoice and be glad in it." (ESV)

Reflections:

1) What do I find myself complaining about most often?

_____

_____

_____

_____

_____

_____

_____

2) What's a different perspective I could take on the things about which I complain?

_____

_____

_____

_____

_____

3) What things am I grateful for in my life?

_____

_____

_____

_____

_____

_____

_____

Prayer: Lord, please forgive me for being so self-centered. Help me to change my perspective on the things that annoy me and exchange my complaining attitude for one of gratefulness. Holy Spirit, I invite You to convict me when I venture into a critical frame of mind, and ask You to help me quickly find the best in my situation and in others. In Jesus Name.

Action Step(s)

_____

_____

_____

_____

_____

_____

_____

CREATIVE WORSHIP

"Jesus said to her, 'I am the resurrection and the life. Those who believe in Me, even though they die, will live, and everyone who lives and believes in Me will never die.'"

John 11:25-26

12 BROKEN FOR YOU

Tonight, I am remembering.....

"When the hour came, He reclined *at the table*, and the apostles with Him. And He said to them, "I have eagerly desired to eat this Passover with you before I suffer; for I say to you, I shall not eat it *again* until it is fulfilled in the kingdom of God." And when He had taken a cup *and* given thanks, He said, "Take this and share it among yourselves; for I say to you, I will not drink of the fruit of the vine from now on until the kingdom of God comes." And when He had taken *some* bread *and* given thanks, He broke it and gave it to them, saying, "This is My body, which is being given for you; do this in remembrance of Me." And in the same way He *took* the cup after they had eaten, saying, "This cup, which is poured out for you, is the new covenant in My blood."(Luke 22:14-20)

Soon after this, Jesus would be betrayed, denied, and abandoned by those closest to Him: His disciples. He was left to walk the unfathomable journey to the cross alone.

My first inclination is to think, "How could His disciples have possibly deserted Him after spending three years of their lives hearing His teaching; watching Him perform miracles, seeing people set free, and watching lives be transformed (including their own!)? How could they run out on Jesus during His darkest hour?"

But then....

How often have I betrayed my Savior by pursuing my own desires rather than His? How often have I denied His Lordship in my life through my thoughtless words and actions?   How often have I abandoned Him by not standing up for my faith more vehemently in the face of adversity?

Tonight I will cast no stones, but instead I will remember. I will humbly ask for forgiveness.

And then I will receive the forgiveness that He shed His blood to provide for me...for us! I will not waste even one drop! Because unlike the disciples, I know the end of this story!

The enemy of our soul is defeated! The sting of death is no more! And there is now no condemnation for those in Christ Jesus!

I'm remembering and repenting (ie. changing the way I think). I'm inviting Holy Spirit to take these next few days to correct me and help me crucify my flesh.

I'm leaving my burial clothes behind, and I'm stepping into God's forgiveness and the Resurrection Power of my Savior. And then, for me, it's game on!

Scripture References:

Romans 8:1 "So now there is no condemnation for those who belong to Christ Jesus." (NLT)

Hebrews 4:15 "For we do not have a high priest who is unable to sympathize with our weaknesses, but One who in every respect has been tempted as we are, yet without sin." (ESV)

Matthew 7:1-3 "Don't judge others, or you will be judged. You will be judged in the same way that you judge others, and the amount you give to others will be given to you. Why do you notice the little piece of dust in your friend's eye, but you don't notice the big piece of wood in your own eye?" (NCV)

Reflections:

1) Do I need to forgive someone for judging me without mercy?

_____

_____

_____

_____

_____

_____

_____

2) Have I judged someone, or a situation, without extending mercy?

_____

_____

_____

_____

_____

3) Who do I need to forgive, or from whom do I need to ask forgiveness?

_____

_____

_____

_____

_____

_____

_____

Prayer: Lord, please forgive me for the times when my thoughts, words, and actions have betrayed Your love and commands. Forgive me for my self-righteousness and my immaturity as I've stood in judgment of others' and their situations. Forgive me for being quick to point out others' weaknesses, while neglecting my own inadequacies. Today I receive Your forgiveness and ask You to align my perspective with Yours', so that going forward I might better reflect Your goodness to those around me. In Jesus Name!

Action Step(s)

_____

_____

_____

_____

_____

_____

CREATIVE WORSHIP

"*You will keep in perfect peace those whose minds are steadfast,
because they trust in You.*"

Isaiah 26:3

13 STORMS OF LIFE

Today was hard! I mean REALLY HARD!

Kind of like the thunderstorms currently surrounding my father's house, so are the myriad of emotional storms invading the tender places of my heart and the deepest parts of my soul.

BUT

In this moment, I am choosing to stir my faith and remind myself, this is just that: a season AND this season WILL pass!

I am reminding myself that no matter how suddenly or unexpectedly the storms of this life might arrive on my doorstep, and no matter how severe or devastating their impact might be, they cannot steal my peace!

The truth is we have been given the authority to speak to the storms of this life and command them TO BE STILL! Just as Jesus spoke to the storm in the book of Matthew, so can we speak to the turmoil happening within our soul!

"Then he got into the boat and his disciples followed him. Suddenly a furious storm came up on the lake, so that the waves swept over the boat. But Jesus was sleeping. The disciples went and woke him, saying, "Lord, save us! We're going to drown!" He replied, "You of little faith, why are you so afraid?" Then he got up and rebuked the winds and the waves, and it was completely calm. The men were amazed and asked, "What kind of man is this? Even the winds and the waves obey him!" Matthew 8:23-27

Instead of reacting in fear, pain, or anger to the trials found hiding in the tumultuous clouds of our inner storms, we can join our faith with our prayers. We can expect God's redeeming love to heal and restore our souls, while seeing us through every overwhelming wave the enemy might send our way!

Tonight I'm choosing to step out of my pain and into the authority of Christ! I am declaring that I will not succumb to any squall raging around or within me! I'm purposing to NOT let my pain, confusion, and fear drown my faith.

Instead, I'm asking Holy Spirit to enable me to take every thought captive while telling every dark, menacing cloud that is attempting to overturn my peace to be gone in Jesus Name!

Ultimately, we MUST remember that there is no weapon that can be formed against us that will prosper. We must remember that we are Daughters of the

King and have the full authority of Christ to overcome every challenge we might face in this world. We are, in fact, more than conquerors, and we are blessed with hope and a beautiful future. Instead of focusing on the storms that are attempting to consume our soul, let's place our focus on Christ and trust Him to work everything together for our good! That's His promise and He is more than trustworthy!

Scripture References:

I Peter 5:10 "And the God of all grace, who called you to His eternal glory in Christ, after you have suffered a little while, will Himself restore you and make you strong, firm and steadfast." (NIV)

Psalm 34:18 "The LORD is close to the brokenhearted and saves those who are crushed in spirit." (NIV)

Isaiah 43:2 "When you pass through the waters, I will be with you; and when you pass through the rivers, they will not sweep over you. When you walk through the fire, you will not be burned; the flames will not set you ablaze." (NIV)

Romans 8:37 "No, in all these things we are more than conquerors through him who loved us." (NIV)

Reflections:

1) What storm within me do I need to release to God?

_____

_____

_____

_____

_____

_____

_____

2) What are God's promises to me when I walk through difficult times?

_____

_____

_____

_____

_____

_____

3) How can I place my focus on God rather than the storm raging within me?

_____

_____

_____

_____

_____

Prayer: Lord, I need You to calm the storm within me. I am filled with fear and heartache, and am overwhelmed by the unknowns. Help me to trust Your promise to restore me and make me strong, firm, and steadfast. Help me to remember that I am more than a conqueror, and I can pass through these raging waters and they will not sweep over me, nor will the fire burn me. I choose today to completely trust You with my heart and my future. In Jesus Name.

Action Step(s)

_____

_____

_____

_____

_____

_____

CREATIVE WORSHIP

"I am the vine; you are the branches. If you remain in Me and I in you, you will bear much fruit; apart from Me you can do nothing."

John 15:5

14 A KISS FROM HEAVEN

The last week has been tough, so I came to sit under my dreaming tree. Set in the middle of the most beautiful meadow, it's where I often retreat when I want to spend some alone time with God without distraction.

There is a cool breeze caressing my face, and I hear the sounds of nature whispering all around me. As I listen, I tell my soul to be quiet, be still, and to listen for that still, small voice.

I long to hear from the One that comforts my soul, the One that lights my path, and the One that pushes darkness back.

How sweet is His Presence! Like honey dripping from its comb, it satisfies my soul.

As I look up, I see the beautiful canopy of leaves and branches covering me, even as God shades me in His nurturing love. I slowly turn my eyes to the horizon where the rich, green tree line lives. I can hear rolling thunder in the distance. A few stray raindrops have escaped the clouds gathering above and land gently on my face.

A kiss from Heaven…

Though my heart is troubled today, I cannot help but worship my King. The One who knows me so very well. The One who knows the beginning from the end. The One who has promised to never leave me, nor forsake me! The One who left heaven, and clothed Himself in flesh for my redemption, my restoration, and my healing!

I am once again reminded that no matter what trial I walk through, I can always run to Him who is faithful!

Despite the challenges of this life, this week, this day, this hour…I declare in this moment, it is well with my soul! I am renewed in His Presence, restored by His Word, and healed by His stripes.

I take a breath and stir my faith, fully expecting Him to work all things together for my good! This is what I know to be true of His Word and true of Who I KNOW Him to be!

So no matter what you're walking through, you can expect no less! Remember, you are a child of the Most High God. You are never alone! Stay the course. He has gone before you and is preparing the way. The way to Him is the way to His perfect destiny for you!

Scripture References:

Psalm 96:12 "Let the fields be jubilant, and everything in them; let all the trees of the forest sing for joy." (NIV)

Psalm 19:1 "The heavens declare the glory of God; the skies proclaim the work of His hands." (NIV)

Psalm 33:5 "The LORD loves righteousness and justice; the earth is full of His unfailing love." (NIV)

John 16:22 "So you have sorrow now, but I will see you again; then you will rejoice, and no one can rob you of that joy." (NLT)

Psalm 33:22 "Let Your unfailing love surround us, Lord, for our hope is in You alone." (NLT)

Psalm 62:5-8 "Yes, my soul, find rest in God; my hope comes from Him. Truly He is my rock and my salvation; He is my fortress, I will not be shaken." (NIV)

Matthew 13:16 "But blessed are your eyes because they see, and your ears because they hear." (NIV)

Reflections:

1) Do I need to get away from the distractions pursuing me and spend some alone time with God? How can I do that?

_____

_____

_____

_____

_____

_____

_____

2) As I reflect on my life, where can I see God working around me?

_____

_____

_____

_____

_____

_____

3) What can I do to stir my faith and keep God's perspective in front of me?

_____

_____

_____

_____

_____

_____

Prayer: Lord, I am so grateful for Your promise to never leave me, nor forsake me. And though I may not always immediately recognize it, I know You are always working around me and for my benefit. Give me eyes to see what You see and ears to hear Your still small voice. Give me a renewed confidence in Your promises and the knowledge of Your unfailing love that always surrounds me. Help me remember that You have gone before me and are perfectly preparing the way for me. I love You, Lord, and I will trust in You without reserve. In Jesus Name.

Action Step(s)

_____

_____

_____

_____

_____

_____

CREATIVE WORSHIP

"Ask and it will be given to you; seek and you will find; knock and the door will be opened to you. For everyone who asks receives; the one who seeks finds; and to the one who knocks, the door will be opened."

Matthew 7:7-8

15 HIGHER GROUND

I have this picture that sits on my dresser that dates back to my Senior year in High School. Soooo long ago!

Seriously, when I look at that picture, I think how I never in a million years would have dreamed that I would be once again living in my childhood room at this stage in my life! "If I knew then what I know now…."

It reminds me how I used to wish God would just tell me what was ahead already. Boy, am I now grateful that He only shares with me on a need-to-know basis! Otherwise…

I've definitely experienced a lot since those early years. Some things have been incredibly exciting, and others have been incredibly exhausting; doors of opportunity swung wide open, and other doors slammed tightly shut; indescribable joy that was often followed by pain beyond description; moments that were planned with the utmost of care, and others have completely caught me off guard.

Through it all, I've come to realize how important it is for me to stay grounded in my relationship with God. He is my Rock, the same yesterday, today, and forever. How incredibly comforting that is when living in a world that is forever-changing!

The truth is life rarely goes exactly as planned. This is especially frustrating for us A-type personalities! However, I know that God has gone before me and prepared my path. I know He will never leave me nor forsake me. I know He has been my anchor and the One who always gives me the courage to just keep moving forward, no matter what life throws at me. I know these things and so much more have enabled me to defeat so many giants in my life!

I realize I will never truly know what each day will bring in the weeks, months, and years to come. Will they be days filled with leaps into my destiny, or will they be days that cause me to dig deep so that I'm able to make even the tiniest of baby steps forward? I honestly don't know the answer to these questions. But what I do know is that Jesus will be there waiting for me and ready to walk me through whatever unfolds…as it unfolds.

Therein lies my peace, and my hope!

So heads UP my friends! Look to the hills, to the Lord, the Giver of our strength. He is ready to secure our footing on higher ground. He is ready to draw us closer to Him! He is ready to guide our footsteps and walk with us every step of the way!

So be of good cheer! Count it ALL joy. Knowing nothing is lost, the good and the seemingly not so good, when you walk with the Lord! You've got this! More importantly God's got us!

Scripture References:

Psalm 139:15-16 "My frame was not hidden from You when I was made in the secret place, when I was woven together in the depths of the earth. Your eyes saw my unformed body; all the days ordained for me were written in Your book." (NIV)

James 1:2-3 "Consider it pure joy, my brothers and sisters, whenever you face trials of many kinds, because you know that the testing of your faith produces perseverance." (NIV)

2 Corinthians 12:9 "But he said to me, "My grace is sufficient for you, for My power is made perfect in weakness." Therefore I will boast all the more gladly about my weaknesses, so that Christ's power may rest on me." (NIV)

Psalm 121:1-3 "I look up to the hills, but where does my help come from? My help comes from the Lord, who made heaven and earth. He will not let you be defeated. He who guards you never sleeps." (NCV)

Reflections:

1) In what areas of my life do I need to release control and trust God?

_____

_____

_____

_____

_____

_____

_____

_____

_____

_____

2) Where or who am I looking to for my strength and direction other than God?

_____

_____

_____

_____

_____

_____

3) What difficulties in my life do I need God to help me reframe so I can see the good in it?

_____

_____

_____

_____

_____

_____

Prayer: Father, please help me to release control of my future and the people in it. Forgive me when I've looked to others for my peace and my security. I ask You to continue reminding me that You formed me in the secret places and have designed the perfect plan for my future. I will look to You alone for my help going forward. I will stand on Your promise to never let me be defeated. With every trial I face, help me count it all joy, knowing You are using it to strengthen my faith and produce perseverance within me. I know I've got this, because You've got me. In Jesus Name.

Action Step(s)

_____

_____

_____

_____

CREATIVE WORSHIP

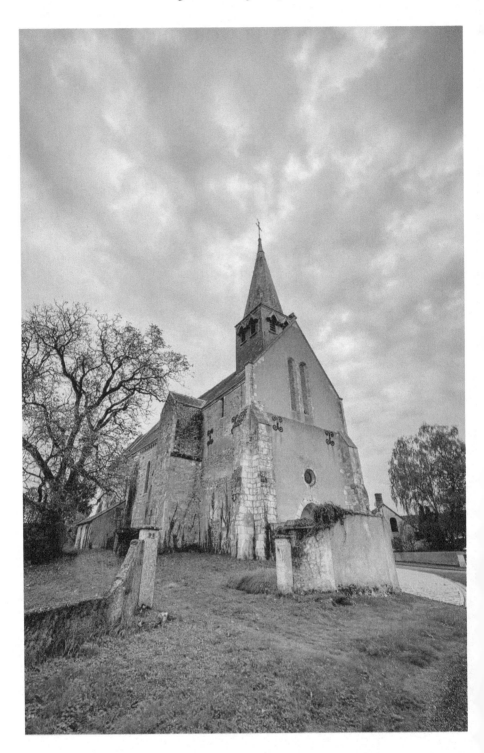

"*I rejoiced with those who said to me,*
'*Let us go to the house of the Lord.*'"

Psalm 122:1

16 MINEFIELDS

I posted a picture on social media today of me refreshing my "look." Yep, I was sitting under a hair dryer with foils in my hair! I remember before my breast cancer journey, I would have never shown a behind-the-scenes look at my personal "beauty regimen!" Just like many others, I much prefer showing my "put-together" side.

It was during my fight to overcome breast cancer, or honestly it probably began during the battle I walked through immediately before (another story for another day) that I began to realize how little my "looks" really matter compared to who I am on the inside!

I've heard it said that one of the greatest prisons people live in is the fear of what other people think of them.

I totally believe that could be true! Why we give other people's opinions so much power over us is quite surprising, yet probably more common than we might think! I know during different seasons I have been guilty of this way of thinking, and it DOES feel like being in a prison of complete torment!

When we worry about what people think about us…our looks, skills, gifts, relationships, jobs, ministry, decisions, our success (or lack thereof), fill-in-the-blank, we set ourselves up for heartache and destructive thinking.

Misplaced expectations, whether introduced by ourselves or others, equals tiptoeing through a minefield of opinions never knowing when the next painful explosion might occur!

I have found the safest, best, and most rewarding place to be is positioned humbly before the throne of my Heavenly Father! He created me. He knows me better than I know myself. He keeps me from thinking more highly of myself than I ought, while ensuring that I know I am so highly treasured that He sent His Only Son to die for me in spite of my many flaws!

The truth is we are all marred with many flaws if we are honest with ourselves. And it is only through God's gracious molding corrections, which will most likely include an ouch here and there, that we are able to come into our true identity. With each correction, if we allow it, we come to know God more intimately and become more secure in who He has created us to be.

His Word tells us that He corrects those He loves: those He calls His sons and daughters. If we can absorb this truth into our hearts, we will soon begin to realize that it is through His correction that He demonstrates His concern for us while setting us free from those things that actually cause us harm. I personally have discovered over the years that it has been during some of my most difficult times in life that I have been most able to grasp God's love for me.

Just as a parent corrects their child to protect them from their often selfish and immature motives, so God corrects us. If we can train ourselves to remain humble and teachable during times of testing, we will not only experience God's unfathomable love, but also deliverance, breakthrough and a spiritual makeover without comparison.

Scripture References:

Proverbs 3:11-12 "My son, do not despise the LORD's discipline, and do not resent His rebuke, because the LORD disciplines those He loves, as a father the son He delights in." (NIV)

Jeremiah 18:2-4 "Go down to the potter's house, and there I will give you my message." So I went down to the potter's house, and I saw him working at the wheel. But the pot he was shaping from the clay was marred in his hands; so the potter formed it into another pot, shaping it as seemed best to him." (NIV)

Reflections:

1) What areas in my life are suffering because I'm too worried about what others might think?

_____

_____

_____

_____

_____

_____

_____

2) In what areas of my life am I being unteachable?

_____

_____

_____

_____

_____

_____

_____

3) Do I struggle with receiving correction from God? From others? Why?

_____

_____

_____

_____

_____

_____

Prayer: Father, forgive me for allowing others' opinions of me and my situation to carry more weight than Yours. Forgive me when I have been prideful and unteachable. Help me to see Your correction as Your way of protecting me and showing me Your love. Help me to remember Your discipline is not rejection as I have often viewed it. I want to be more humble and more teachable that I might be more like You. Mold me and shape me as it seems best to You. I want my life to bring glory to Your name. Today I choose to surrender my will and my future to You. In Jesus Name.

Action Step(s)

_____

_____

_____

_____

_____

_____

CREATIVE WORSHIP

"For God, who said, 'Let light shine out of darkness,' made His light shine in our hearts to give us the light of the knowledge of God's glory displayed in the face of Christ."

2 Corinthians 4:6

17 TIME FOR A CHECK-UP

I'm waiting in the lobby for my daddy. He's got a check-up with the doctor today.

As I'm sitting here, I'm thinking how important it is to never neglect not only our physical check-ups, but also our spiritual ones!

Life is full of ups and downs. There are days when we may feel like we're on the highest of mountaintops, and on other days we may find ourselves trudging through the deepest valleys! The loss of a relationship, a dream unrealized, an unexpected diagnosis, a mislaid accusation, or disappointment in a promise made are just some of the things that can so quickly steal our joy.

As we all know, we live in a fallen world, filled with broken people. Painful moments are simply, and unfortunately, inevitable.

BUT

It is during these painful moments in life that we all have the opportunity to take our wounds to the throne room of God where He works miracles as only He can!

The Truth is Jesus has purchased our healing with His shed blood on the cross. His healing salve is always available to heal those places where our deepest hurts and disappointments lie!

Today, while doing my "spiritual check-up," I'm reminding myself of these things. Whether I'm on the highest mountaintop celebrating or in the valley of the darkest despair, I can place my every situation into the hands of God.

No matter the pain of an unfounded accusation, no matter the unexpected misunderstanding or the barrage of hurtful words, no matter the unrealized dreams or frightening diagnosis, Jesus has gone before me and will walk me safely through whatever it is I'm facing.

And with each encounter and every experience, it is my deepest desire to take every situation to the throne of God. It is here that He can help me take responsibility for my actions and extend mercy and forgiveness freely to those who have hurt me intentionally or unintentionally.

My hope will forever remain in Jesus, Who is faithful without fail. He is faithful to heal. He is faithful to restore. He is faithful to raise every valley, to bring every mountain low, and to cause my way to be made straight. He takes the rough places and makes them like a plain. Truly Jesus is faithful in EVERY imaginable way!

So no matter what ails you today physically, spiritually, or emotionally, you can KNOW Jesus came to cure the sick and poor in spirit, heal our souls, restore our relationships, and to provide for our every need. Jesus is the Great Physician; therefore, we can be at peace.

Scripture References:

Mark 2:17 "Jesus said to them, 'It is not the healthy who need a doctor, but the sick. I have not come to call the righteous, but sinners.'" (NIV)

Jeremiah 30:17 "'But I will restore you to health and heal your wounds,' declares the LORD." (NIV)

Isaiah 40:4 "Every valley shall be raised up, every mountain and hill made low; the rough ground shall become level, the rugged places a plain." (NIV)

2 Thessalonians 3:3 "But the Lord is faithful, and He will strengthen you and protect you from the evil one." (NIV)

Isaiah 45:2-6 "I will go before you and will level the mountains; I will break down gates of bronze and cut through bars of iron. I will give you hidden treasures, riches stored in secret places, so that you may know that I am the LORD, the God of Israel, who summons you by name." (NIV)

Reflections:

1) What concerns do I need to place in the hands of God today?

_____

_____

_____

_____

_____

_____

_____

_____

_____

2) What do I need to take responsibility for in my life? Who do I need to forgive and extend mercy to for their hurtful words or actions?

_____

_____

_____

_____

_____

_____

3) Where do I need Jesus to place His healing salve in my life?

_____

_____

_____

_____

_____

Prayer: Lord, I ask that You would restore my health and heal my wounds. Help me to meditate on Your promises and receive the healing You purchased for me on the cross. I ask that Your love would invade my heart and my every circumstance. I'm trusting You to lift up my valleys of despair while lowering the ominous mountains that desire to overtake me. Make the rugged places plain and shine Your light brightly upon my path. I know You are placing Your healing salve in the wounds of my soul, while restoring and renewing me as only You can. I invite Your joy to be my strength this day and every day going forward. In Jesus name.

Action Step(s)

_____

_____

_____

_____

_____

CREATIVE WORSHIP

"For we live by faith, not by sight."

2 Corinthians 5:7

18 THREE DRESSES FOR EASTER

I had been serving at the church for some time and creating artistic expressions as sermon illustrations. I also had started assisting with the programming of all weekend services. I absolutely loved being able to use my theatrical background to serve the One I loved most! It was an absolute dream come true, and I knew it was exactly where God wanted me to be!

As we were approaching Easter weekend one year, my pastors asked me to join them on the platform to lead during one of the ministry segments. I was shocked, honored, scared, excited…and didn't have anything to wear! Seriously, since I had left my job as a personnel director for an aerospace company in Phoenix, my finances had been very slim and I hadn't bought a new outfit in over a year. Plus, I had given most of my "professional" clothing away.

So the search for something appropriate to wear on the platform for Easter morning began. Due to my very limited budget, I started at Ross and TJ Maxx. And not just one of them, many of them. After several days of searching, I was unable to find ONE dress that was within my budget that actually fit. I was really beginning to stress out!

I remember talking with a friend and expressing my concern. We decided the next day we would hit every Goodwill within the Phoenix metro area. I HAD to find something and quickly. That night I prayed, "Lord, I believe You are the One giving me this assignment and You know my need. Would You direct us tomorrow and help me find a dress suitable for Easter Sunday? One that's actually within my budget? In Jesus Name, Amen."

The next morning I overslept and was running around like a crazy woman when I noticed through my living room window that someone had just pulled up in front of the house. It wasn't my friend, and I didn't recognize the car. I saw a woman get out and reach into the back of her car to retrieve something. I didn't know who she was, and I couldn't tell what it was she was carrying, but she was walking towards my front door.

As I opened the door, I realized I had seen her before leading worship at our church. I didn't really know her. In fact, I'm embarrassed to say I couldn't remember her name. So I did the extended, "Hiiii" greeting you give when you can't say, "Hi, so and so!"

She smiled and told me, "Early this morning when I was praying, the Lord instructed me to go to my closet and He had me select these three dresses for you. He said I was to deliver them to you early this morning." Even as I'm writing this tears are starting to stream down my face…just as they did in that moment over 30 years ago. I was so overwhelmed that I literally ran to my room and fell on my knees thanking God for His beautiful and extravagant gift. I literally just left her standing in my doorway holding the dresses!! I still can't believe I did that, but I was just so overwhelmed by what had just happened! Once I realized what I had done, I ran back both apologizing and thanking her profusely. I told her of my situation, and she cried as well. It was the most beautiful moment and is forever sealed in my heart.

I wore one of those three dresses that Easter Sunday, and the others I wore in the coming weeks as more and more opportunities to minister from the platform came. I received so many compliments on my dress that weekend and literally EVERY time I wore one of "God's dresses!" I especially remember people saying, "That dress looks like it was made for you." And every time I was able to say, "Oh, this dress is from my Father," and share my story.

Never will I forget this special gift. Not just my beautiful dresses (which I still have), but the gift God planted in my heart that day. His incredible love and indescribable concern for what concerns us is without end. It was true for me and it is true for you…if only you invite Him into the secret parts of your life. He's waiting to surprise you, too!

Scripture References:

Philippians 4:19 "And my God shall supply all your need according to His riches in glory by Christ Jesus." (NKJV)

Reflections:

1) What need(s) do I need to turn over to God?

_____

_____

_____

_____

_____

_____

_____

_____

_____

2) What lies am I believing concerning my personal needs?

_____

_____

_____

_____

_____

_____

3) What is the Truth that counters every lie I'm believing?

_____

_____

_____

_____

_____

Prayer: Lord, I invite You into the intimate parts of my heart today. You already know where I have fear, where I'm not trusting You, and where I have need. You know the beginning from the end and everything in between. Worrying about my physical, spiritual, emotional, and financial needs will do nothing to change my circumstances. But I know that if I place these things into Your hands, entrusting You to take care of each of them exactly how and when You think is best, my heart can rest in Your perfect peace. So today I choose to trust You, Lord, and release my every worry and need to Your care. In Jesus Name.

Action Step(s)

_____

_____

_____

_____

_____

_____

CREATIVE WORSHIP

"The Lord Himself goes before you and will be with you; He will never leave you nor forsake you. Do not be afraid; do not be discouraged."

Deuteronomy 31:8

19 UNDER THE DREAMING TREE

Today I moved my dreaming bench under the dreaming tree. I love that my place of reflection is now shaded by the overarching branches of this 250+ year-old oak tree!

As I was dreaming about restored lives, relationships, families, and the future, I was reminded how life can sometimes throw us some pretty intense curve balls. Some are more painful than others, some come out of the blue, and some are completely designed by the enemy to take us off the course God has designed for our lives.

Usually these seasons of turmoil circulate around relationships with family, friends, co-workers, etc. When these unexpected storms dust up, I have found it is imperative that I keep my eyes INTENTLY on Jesus! If I focus too much of my attention on what is happening TO me, replaying scenarios over and over in my mind, I run the risk of putting myself into the judgment seat (not my place to occupy) and missing out on what God wants to do IN me.

You see, part of my gift mix includes "storytelling" which has allowed me to create MANY shows and experiences over the years. It has been a huge blessing for me and I hope for many others!

BUT it has also been my greatest weakness when it has not been submitted to the Giver of the gift! I have often allowed one thought to lead to another and before I know it an innocent incident has evolved into a full-blown drama! (Let's keep the drama on the stage where it belongs!)

When I allow my imagination to move me from reality to perceptions grounded in emotions, I set myself and those around me up for unnecessary heartache.

My challenge I believe will always be to ensure my *gifting* doesn't lead me and my choices. Instead it is imperative that the Giver of my gift (GOD) leads me at all times. If I don't do this, I run the risk of being ensnared in deception, which entices destruction rather than Truth that promotes healing!

The bottom line, when in a trial of any kind, we need to make sure our eyes stay on Jesus more than our problems. He is masterful at maneuvering us through every curve in our sometimes emotionally bumpy road, while ensuring we make it to the other side without stumbling.

It is also important that our gifts always remain yielded to their Giver. The reality is, no matter how gifted we might happen to be, our gifts have been given to us that we might serve others and administer God's grace. Our gifts are not our Savior, but FOR our Savior!

Lastly, it is so important that we don't get stuck. Breakthrough often arrives as we break forward. This means we have to let go of the past in order to move forward and "through" our challenges! There can be no settling in! Hope, healing, restoration, and victory is where God desires to lead us, but to be led we must be willing to go, even if it's baby step by baby step. #justkeepmovingmovingmoving

Scripture References:

Psalm 71:20 "Though You have made me see troubles, many and bitter, You will restore my life again; from the depths of the earth You will again bring me up." (NIV)

Matthew 7:1-2 "Do not judge, or you too will be judged. For in the same way you judge others, you will be judged, and with the measure you use, it will be measured to you." (NIV)

I Peter 4:10 "Each one should use whatever gift he has received to serve others, faithfully administering God's grace in its various forms." (NIV)

Jude 1:24-25 "To Him who is able to keep you from stumbling and to present you before His glorious presence without fault and with great joy." (NIV)

Jeremiah 17:9 "The heart is deceitful above all things and beyond cure. Who can understand it?" (NIV)

Reflections:

1) Where in my life do I need to redirect my focus to Jesus?

_____

_____

_____

_____

_____

_____

_____

_____

2) In what areas am I placing my confidence in my gifts, rather than in God?

_____

_____

_____

_____

_____

_____

_____

3) Where am I stuck? How can I move forward?

_____

_____

_____

_____

_____

_____

Prayer: Father, forgive me for the times when I have given my problems more power and attention than I have given to You. Forgive me for the times when I've allowed my gifts and strengths to be my Savior, rather than looking to You for guidance and deliverance. Forgive me for the times when I have thought that I knew better than You and stepped unrightfully into the place as judge over my circumstances and those around me. Lord, please consume any pride within me, cause my gaze to be upon You only, and stir my gifts for Your glory and the benefit of others. In Jesus Name.

Action Step(s)

_____

_____

_____

_____

_____

_____

_____

CREATIVE WORSHIP

"*He gives me new strength. He leads me on paths that are right for the good of His name. Even if I walk through a very dark valley, I will not be afraid, because You are with me. Your rod and Your shepherd's staff comfort me.*"

Psalm 23:3-4

20 DANIEL'S SONG

It was the middle of the night when I suddenly and abruptly woke up. My water had broken! But why?!? I was only six months pregnant! Needless to say, fear completely gripped my heart in this moment as I shook my husband out of a dead sleep. We had to get to the hospital!

We arrived at the emergency room and were quickly taken in for an ultrasound. I remember it being so dark in the room. Unlike the many times before at our ultrasound visits, this time there was no excitement. In fact, we couldn't even see the screen, though I do remember hearing my baby's heartbeat. The ultrasound technician left right after the test was done, and we sat in the dark room waiting. There were no words spoken, just silence as we waited for the doctor to come and tell us what we could expect in the upcoming hours…

I closed my eyes, and the moment I did, I saw a vision begin to quickly unfold. First, I saw the Lord playing with a baby. The child was giggling and so filled with joy as the Lord gently tossed the child up in the air over and over again. Next, I saw myself in a room, on my knees praying and asking the Lord if He would please "tell my baby I love him" (although, at this point I didn't know what we were having). Then, I saw myself standing in a park of sorts. It was beautiful and green with huge oak trees all around. From behind, I saw the Lord sitting with a young child on a bench. I saw Him, with a smile, lean over to the child and I heard him say, "Mommy says she loves you!"

I quickly opened my eyes, because at that moment I knew our baby would not be going home with us that day, but instead home to be with the Lord. I never until that day had experienced so much pain, joy, and peace all at the same time!

I gave birth to a baby boy that day. We named him Daniel. He lived for about 1.5 hours, and I am so grateful for those precious moments to hold and love him before God took him home to live with Him.

In the days that followed, two of my dearest friends, Greg Dille and Marianne Cook, wrote songs about Daniel and my vision. They were both beautiful, anointed, and sung at his funeral. That day will be forever imprinted on my heart as both the hardest and most beautiful day of my life. I worshiped and experienced the presence of God as never before.

I will never forget the Lord's incredible kindness towards me during this season and the beautiful Truths He deposited in my heart. His promise of "the perfect peace that surpasses all understanding" was woven into the fibers of my being that day…never to be taken. A treasure for a treasure.

I want you to know that no matter what it is you're facing right now, God is near and He has a plan to work everything together for good. I promise!

Scripture References:

Philippians 4:6-7 "Do not be anxious about anything, but in every situation, by prayer and petition, with thanksgiving, present your requests to God. And the peace of God, which transcends all understanding, will guard your hearts and your minds in Christ Jesus." (NIV)

Revelation 21:4 "He will wipe away every tear from their eyes, and death shall be no more, neither shall there be mourning, nor crying, nor pain anymore, for the former things have passed away." (ESV)

Proverbs 17:17 "A friend loves at all times, and a brother is born for a time of adversity." (NIV)

John 14:27 "Peace I leave with you; my peace I give you. I do not give to you as the world gives. Do not let your hearts be troubled and do not be afraid." (NIV)

Isaiah 61:2-3 "...to comfort all who mourn, and provide for those who grieve in Zion—to bestow on them a crown of beauty instead of ashes,
the oil of joy instead of mourning, and a garment of praise instead of a spirit of despair. They will be called oaks of righteousness, a planting of the Lord" for the display of his splendor." (NIV)

Reflections:

1) What deep hurts do I still hold on to that I need God to heal?

_____

_____

_____

_____

_____

_____

_____

_____

_____

2) Is there someone I need to forgive? Myself? God?

_____

_____

_____

_____

_____

_____

3) What Truth(s) in God's Word can I apply as a healing salve to my wounds?

_____

_____

_____

_____

_____

_____

Prayer: Father, I bring all of my hurts to You and ask that You would heal them with the balm of Your Word. Help me to forgive and release any who were a part of inflicting my pain, even if I believed that to be me or You. Turn what the enemy meant for evil, my pain and my ashes, into a crown of beauty that will reflect Your glory. I trust that you will neither waste one tear nor ache of my heart, but will instead use each and every one as a platform for me to display Your splendor to the world around me. In Jesus Name!

Action Step(s)

_____

_____

_____

_____

_____

CREATIVE WORSHIP

"He who dwells in the shelter of the Most High will abide in the shadow of the Almighty. I will say to the LORD, 'My refuge and my fortress, my God, in whom I trust.'"

Psalm 91:1-2

21 IN HIS FOOTSTEPS

As I sit reflecting this morning, a Narnia soundtrack plays in the background. A deliciously scented candle flickers on my desk, as the darkness of night escapes to sleep in another part of the world.

This early morning I'm reminded that though we each are given the opportunity to choose our path, God has promised to order our steps. He has said He will go before us and prepare the way. He not only has designed good things for us, but He has also placed us where we can reflect His light and be His ambassadors to those He sets around us. He has called us to be His hands and feet to a world that desperately needs His unconditional love and powerful presence.

As we rest in this truth, we can trust Holy Spirit to lead and direct our footsteps ensuring we will always be "at the right place at the right time."

This week I was photographing an incredibly gorgeous wedding. There was a castle, fireworks, three designer dresses, matching designer shoes, a champagne fountain, and the list goes on. As weddings go, everything was absolutely perfect!

With only thirty minutes left until the grand sparkler exit, the unimaginable happened! Everyone was up dancing when a man sitting at one of the surrounding tables suddenly had a Grand Mal seizure and flatlined.

Not surprisingly, an anxious somberness quickly overshadowed what was only moments before a joyous celebration.

911 was called as an off-duty police officer, with the help of a few other guests, began CPR. As I stood there watching in disbelief, I heard Holy Spirit whisper to me, "Go lay hands on the man and pray for him." I hesitated only a moment before quietly moving around to the foot of the gentleman fighting for his life. Most everyone was focused on those administering CPR and didn't notice when I gently reached out and laid my hand on the man's lower leg and began to quietly pray.

The moment my hand touched his leg, he abruptly and loudly coughed. "He's breathing!" someone exclaimed, and a small wave of relief could be felt throughout the room as tears began to flow down the face of his wife.

As I continued to pray, my hand still on his leg, I had this thought. "Perhaps this is why I'm REALLY here and not simply to photograph a wedding. Perhaps today God needed me to be His ambassador in a moment of great desperation."

Over the next few minutes, the man's pulse slowly began to strengthen as his breathing also steadied. Paramedics arrived shortly after, and he was taken to the hospital. The magnitude of what had just happened suddenly overtook me, and I could no longer choke back the tears. I was in complete awe of what God had just done! I found out later the next day, the man was miraculously released that afternoon. The doctors could not explain his quick recovery.

Today I'm worshiping and celebrating my Father's goodness. I'm filling my mind and heart with His Truth, because who knows where His steps might lead me tomorrow; I want to be ready…in season and out!

Scripture References:

Mark 16:17-18 "And these signs shall follow them that believe; In my name shall they cast out devils; they shall speak with new tongues; They shall take up serpents; and if they drink any deadly thing, it shall not hurt them; they shall lay hands on the sick, and they shall recover." (KJV)

2 Corinthians 5:20 "We are therefore Christ's ambassadors, as though God were making His appeal through us. We implore you on Christ's behalf: Be reconciled to God." (NIV)

2 Timothy 4:2 "Preach the Word; be prepared in season and out of season; correct, rebuke and encourage—with great patience and careful instruction." (NIV)

Reflections:

1) Has God ever asked me to do something I wasn't comfortable doing? If so, what was it and how did I respond?

_____

_____

_____

_____

_____

_____

_____

_____

2) In what areas do I need my faith to grow?

_____

_____

_____

_____

_____

_____

3) How can I better prepare myself for the future, knowing God might call me to step out of my comfort zone to serve Him at any time?

_____

_____

_____

_____

_____

_____

Prayer: Lord, I want my faith to grow so You can call on me at any time in any situation, to represent You. Will you guide me in Your Word, so that my faith and trust in You might grow? Will you give me strength and courage to face any giant that might rise up before me, while reminding me of Your faithfulness and Your promise that signs and wonders will follow me as one of Your disciples? I invite you to teach me how to walk in all of the promises Your Word says are my portion as Your child, while keeping every evil thing from harming me. I'm expectant and excited to be a tool in Your hand and a weapon for the Kingdom of God. In Jesus Name.

Action Step(s)

_____

_____

_____

_____

_____

CREATIVE WORSHIP

"Blessed is the one who perseveres under trial because, having stood the test, that person will receive the crown of life that the Lord has promised to those who love Him."

James 1:12

22 HIS STRENGTH IN MY WEAKNESS

I just want to set the record straight. Over the past months and years, I have often had people say to me, "You're so strong!"

And though that is so nice to think that's what people think of me, the reality is, I am actually VERY weak!

Truth be told, my heart is extremely sensitive, my identity is very fragile, and my hopes and dreams can be easily dashed.

Some of you who know my testimony also know that at one time I was into drugs and even made several lame attempts at suicide by taking handfuls of diet pills. And though I no longer take drugs or attempt to kill myself, I still have to fight some of the weaknesses I mentioned above.

Actually, what some people see as strength is in reality God displaying HIS strength in my weakness! I don't know how He does it, but I am beyond grateful that He does!

So many times I have been found in situations where I am completely "at the end of myself." Too often feelings of hopelessness and desperation have come like a tsunami out of nowhere to wipe me out. But you know what I have discovered? It is when I'm "at the end of myself," that I find myself in the perfect place for God to do His miraculous work both in and through me!

What would, should, or could destroy me, God somehow uses to shake, shape, and mold me into His likeness. Little by little through each and every hardship, I have come to know Him more and more intimately. Through each trial, my trust in Him expands exponentially, and suddenly His strength goes on display! Again, I cannot even begin to explain how He does it! I just know He promises He will, and so He does!

This, for me, is why reading and knowing His Word has become my lifeline.

God's word reminds me of who He is as well as who I am in Him! THIS revelation is where I see His strength rise up within me. It's where Jesus shows up, and makes me "look good." (Wink)

The Truth is, God alone is good, and God alone is truly strong. I just, once in a while, get into the right position (usually on my knees...no actually on my face), and it is during that moment you might get an ever-so-small glimpse of His reflection! In that micro moment, I APPEAR strong. But truthfully, it is Him working in me!

I'm working on staying in that submissive stance more consistently, in hopes that His reflection might be seen just a bit more often and a bit more clearly. Because I know that when people see Him and not me, change, freedom, healing, and salvation are just around the corner. And ultimately isn't that what's most important?

I just wanted to set the record straight!

Scripture References:

Zechariah 4:6 "So He said to me, "This is the word of the Lord to Zerubbabel: 'Not by might nor by power, but by My Spirit,' says the Lord Almighty." (NIV)

2 Corinthians 12:9-10 "But He said to me, "My grace is sufficient for you, for My power is made perfect in weakness." Therefore I will boast all the more gladly about my weaknesses, so that Christ's power may rest on me. That is why, for Christ's sake, I delight in weaknesses, in insults, in hardships, in persecutions, in difficulties. For when I am weak, then I am strong." (NIV)

Isaiah 40:29 "He gives power to the faint, and to him who has no might he increases strength." (ESV)

Psalm 73:26 "My flesh and my heart may fail, but God is the strength of my heart and my portion forever." (NIV)

Reflections:

1) What weaknesses in my life do I need to embrace, so God can display His strength?

_____

_____

_____

_____

_____

_____

_____

_____

_____

2) Where am I placing my confidence in myself rather than the Spirit of God?

_____

_____

_____

_____

_____

_____

3) What areas of my life do I need to submit to God?

_____

_____

_____

_____

_____

_____

Prayer: Father, You see my weaknesses, and they do not surprise You. I don't know why I feel the need to hide them instead of allowing you to shine through them. Help me to remember that You have confirmed through Your Word, multiple times, that You will provide for my every need. You have told me that nothing shall be accomplished through my own might nor power, but by Your Spirit alone. I receive Your grace, which is more than sufficient. I thank You that Your power is made perfect in my weakness. It is IN my weakness that Your power will rest upon me. I will delight in my hardships and difficulties, knowing in these Your strength and power may be displayed in my life. In Jesus Name.

Action Step(s)

_____

_____

_____

_____

_____

CREATIVE WORSHIP

"The harvest is plentiful but the workers are few. Ask the Lord of the harvest, therefore, to send out workers into His harvest field."

Matthew 9:37-38

23 ANCHORED IN THE STORM

When the storms of life overwhelm us, it can be difficult to get our bearings and to find proper perspective!

One moment the impending darkness threatens to consume us; the next, a ray of light breaks forth chasing that same darkness back into its unrelenting origins.

One moment we're lost, broken, hopeless and defeated. And the next moment our vision is clear, and our passion is strong as we stand upright defying any foe that dare rear its ugly head against us!

It is during these times of instability that there is only one thing that is truly able to stabilize me: the anchor of God's Word!

The reality is we have an enemy that wants to toss us to and fro with lies intended to ravage our souls. Satan wants nothing more than to distract us from the purposes intended for our destiny. He wants to steal our hope, kill our dreams, and destroy our identity. Ominous storms are our enemy's specialty. Usually birthed in illusion and deception, his tactics are distortions of the reality found in God's Truth.

If only we would train ourselves to lift our eyes to Jesus during the barrage of these storms, we would quickly find the extended hand of our Rescuer.

It is in our Rescuer's presence that the storm loses its power AND its momentum! It is in these places of vulnerability that our Savior most often instructs us on how to navigate the jarring and unchartered waters of this life!

As I have continued to train myself to incline my ear to His still small voice during each storm's bombardment, I have more and more quickly seen Him rend the thunderous lies that threaten to capsize my hope and my future.

Part of this process has been learning to take every thought captive and make it obedient to Christ. (If you haven't noticed, this is a recurring theme in my journey!) Ultimately, this is where my perspectives are transformed, and true freedom is realized! It is where His Truth calms my storm and guides me into the harbor of His love and restoration! It's where the storms of life are quieted, and His light permeates my very being. It's where life, though my circumstances may not have changed, is once again good.

If you are currently facing a storm in your life, know Jesus has His hand extended and is ready to come to your rescue. You need only come near to Him, and He promises to come near to you. This is where His light will most assuredly dispel your storm's darkness and release you from its control!

Scripture References:

John 8:12 "When Jesus spoke again to the people, He said, "I am the light of the world. Whoever follows Me will never walk in darkness, but will have the light of life." (NIV)

Psalm 27:1 "The LORD is my light and my salvation- whom shall I fear? The LORD is the stronghold of my life-of whom shall I be afraid?" (NIV)

Proverbs 3:6 "Listen for God's voice in everything you do, everywhere you go; He's the one who will keep you on track." (MSG)

Psalm 31:24 "Be strong and take heart, all you who hope in the LORD." (NIV)

Psalm 46:1-3 "God is our refuge and strength, always ready to help in times of trouble. So we will not fear when earthquakes come and the mountains crumble into the sea. Let the oceans roar and foam. Let the mountains tremble as the waters surge!" (NLT)

James 4:8 "Come near to God and He will come near to you..." (NIV)

Reflections:

1) Where is the enemy stealing my hope and/or killing my dreams?

_____

_____

_____

_____

_____

_____

_____

_____

_____

2) How has the enemy attempted to destroy my identity?

_____

_____

_____

_____

_____

_____

3) What do I hear God's still small voice saying to me?

_____

_____

_____

_____

_____

_____

Prayer: Though darkness threatens to consume me, I will trust Your light to push it back to its origins. I will listen for Your voice and trust You to order my steps. My hope will remain in You, and I will be strong and take heart. I will lean into You, Lord, and trust You to come near me. You alone are my strength, always ready to help me in times of trouble. You are my salvation, whom shall I fear? I reach for Your hand and await Your valiant rescue. You are worthy of my praise and my trust. I love you Lord and I invite Your Kingdom to come and Your Will to be done. In Jesus Name.

Action Step(s)

_____

_____

_____

_____

_____

_____

CREATIVE WORSHIP

"If I have the gift of prophecy and can fathom all mysteries and all knowledge, and if I have a faith that can move mountains, but do not have love, I am nothing."

1 Corinthians 13:2

24 CHANGING LANDSCAPES

Usually I go for prayer walks in the mornings. Not only is it good exercise, it helps me focus my attention on God before starting my day.

One day while I was still living in Arizona, I had decided to walk down a dirt road a couple of miles from where I was living. I had actually walked by its entrance several times before, but wasn't feeling adventurous enough to take its wandering path. This particular day, I decided to go for it.

After walking down its winding road for about fifteen minutes, the terrain suddenly changed. It was so unexpected! One minute I was walking in a full blown desert landscape surrounded by cactus, and the next I found myself in the middle of what looked like the grasslands of the Midwest?!
I remember thinking, "How strange! Where am I, Auntie Emm?" Haha!

Isn't that how life is sometimes? You choose a path, everything seems to be going per usual, and then without notice your whole landscape changes! Sometimes it's super exciting, and other times it's not so much! I guess when you think about it, life will always involve change.

I know in traveling both in America and abroad, landscapes are so very different, and yet strangely often the same. I've encountered winding roads, and mountains that disappeared into the skies, and treacherous valleys that were miles deep. Some changes were subtle, while others were starkly drastic.

Fortunately, unlike life's terrain, our Heavenly Father's incredible love for us will never change. So as I'm sitting here reflecting in the wee hours of the night, I'm reminding myself of this:

Though the terrain of life continue to change around me, though one day I may find myself on the highest mountaintop and the next in the lowest valley, and though the road be smooth in one instance and uneven and bumpy in the next, I can always rely on the stability of God's Word.

Whether my landscape be beautiful or treacherous, my view limited or expansive, and my scenery beckoning or seemingly sending me away, this is what I know. God's faithfulness will always be constant! He has promised to never leave me nor forsake me. He has assured me that He will order my each and every step, and without a doubt I know, I can trust Him in ALL things.

So though one day I find myself walking in a desert and the next running through green lush meadows, I will be at peace. I know that regardless of my situation, God is cultivating the terrain of my heart. And when He is done with landscaping my heart, it won't matter where the road of this life takes me, because I will then have the ability to see my terrain through my Father's eyes.

Scripture References:

Psalm 51:10 "Create in me a pure heart, O God, and renew a steadfast spirit within me." (NIV)

Proverbs 3:6 "In all your ways acknowledge Him, And He will make your paths straight." (NAS)

Psalm 36:5 "Your love, Lord, reaches to the heavens, Your faithfulness to the skies." (NIV)

Deuteronomy 31:8 "Do not be afraid or discouraged, for the Lord will personally go ahead of you. He will be with you; He will neither fail you nor abandon you." (NLT)

Psalm 119:133 "Establish my footsteps in [the way of] Your word; Do not let any human weakness have power over me [causing me to be separated from You]." (Amplified)

Psalm 119:18 "Open my eyes to see the miracles in your teachings." (NCV)

Reflections:

1) Is the ever-changing terrain of my life, or God, directing the attitudes of my heart?

_____

_____

_____

_____

_____

_____

_____

_____

2) What areas of my heart do I need the Lord to restore?

_____

_____

_____

_____

_____

_____

_____

3) Where in my life do I need to see my circumstances through my Heavenly Father's eyes?

_____

_____

_____

_____

_____

_____

Prayer: Though the terrain of my life continues to change, Lord I will place my faith in the constancy of Your love and Your promise to never leave me nor forsake me. Give me eyes to see and create in me a pure heart. Renew a steadfast spirit within me, as I acknowledge You in all my ways. I will stand on Your promises and rest in the fact that You have gone before me and will make my path straight. Keep fear and discouragement far from me, as I follow in the footsteps of Your Word. My heart is at peace, knowing that You are forever with me until the end of time. In Jesus Name.

Action Step(s)

_____

_____

_____

_____

_____

CREATIVE WORSHIP

"The Lord is my rock, my fortress and my deliverer; my God is my rock, in whom I take refuge, my shield and the horn of my salvation, my stronghold."

Psalm 18:2

25 I HEARD HIS VOICE

I had only just committed my life to following Christ, so "this fish needed a LOT of cleaning!" I pretty much joined every group available and was at the church every moment its doors opened. I was so hungry for the truth and so very in love with Jesus. He had literally come after me during the darkest time in my life and lavished me with His unconditional love. All I wanted to do was learn more about Him and become more and more like Him.

One of the first Bible studies I joined was one with a group of young women from the Singles Ministry. I remember one evening we were doing a study on forgiveness. I don't remember exactly what was said that night, but I do remember me realizing I had unforgiveness in my heart.

For years my mom and I had struggled in our relationship. When I wasn't around her, I would think how much I loved and appreciated her; but the moment I heard her voice, something physically would tighten in my chest and I would shut her out. Oh, we could exchange pleasantries, but anything beyond often turned into a heated argument. I hated it, and I hated the way I felt. We both were aware of the discomfort, but just couldn't seem to overcome it.

During the Bible study that night, I began to realize unforgiveness was at the root of our problem. At the close of the lesson, we were invited to spend some time journaling. During that time, I realized I had made judgments towards my mom that were related to my daddy.

My dad worked long hours and when he came home, I wanted nothing more than to sit in his lap and hear his voice. However, there were times this was interrupted with *lively discussions*, that infringed on my special time with Daddy.

As an adult, I realize disagreements are unfortunately a normal thing between a husband and wife, but as a child I resented the interruptions. And there was the rare occasion (ok, maybe not so rare haha) I was "told on," and Daddy had to address my transgressions. (That's actually kind of funny to me now, but it wasn't back then.) I felt like mom was "stealing" my time and my relationship with my daddy. (Isn't it crazy how things get twisted in our minds?!)

During my journaling time that night, I realized I had blamed my mom for the loss of every treasured moment with my dad. I also realized I had made vows in my heart against her. As I was writing this all down, I heard these words pop into my mind, "Stop It!" It was so distinct that I actually stopped my journaling and looked around the room. Obviously no one had said it, but I had definitely heard those words. Deciding to move on, I resumed my journaling and knew I had to call my mom, and forgive her.

The next day I called and started the awkward conversation. I was so concerned about hurting my mom's feelings, it took awhile to get out what I wanted to say. I knew this was MY issue, not hers, but I needed to explain what God had shown me. As I recanted my disdain with her and daddy's *exchanges*, I clarified this was my viewpoint as a child, and I didn't want her to feel bad. I wanted to own my unforgiveness! She was deathly quiet as I spoke, and all I could think was, "I've hurt her." I felt terrible.

Then she spoke, her voice breaking. "I remember this one time when your father and I were arguing." I asked her to go on. She said, "It was rather heated, and you got so upset. You ran to your room yelling, 'Stop it, Stop it, Stop it!' You were only about three years old, but you must have said those words over and over for an hour or more." I suddenly remembered how those exact words had interrupted my journaling the night before. "Stop It!" I immediately heard the Lord say, "This is when it started. You made a vow in your heart and bitterness took root."

My mom and I both cried that day as God began the process of healing our hearts and our relationship. And though we still had a journey ahead of us, I never again experienced that physical twisting in my chest. God had done what only He could do.

Scripture References:

Colossians 3:13 "Bear with each other and forgive one another if any of you has a grievance against someone. Forgive as the Lord forgave you." (NIV)

Reflections:

1) What vows do I need to renounce and give to the Lord?

_____

_____

_____

_____

_____

_____

_____

_____

_____

2) Who do I need to forgive? What situations do I need to give to God?

_____

_____

_____

_____

_____

_____

_____

3) Do I need to address my offender in person, write a letter, or just give it to the Lord in prayer?

_____

_____

_____

_____

_____

_____

Prayer: Lord, You know who I hold offenses against in my heart. Please give me the grace and courage to release their wrong doings (whether actual or perceived) to You. Help me to forgive others as You forgive me. Don't let me procrastinate and not address the things You are bringing to my remembrance. I don't want anything to block me from the many blessings I know You want to bestow upon me. Give me supernatural boldness and divine mercy as I obey your command to forgive. I trust You to set all things right and heal the wounds of those impacted by any offense I have held in my heart. In Jesus Name.

Action Step(s)

_____

_____

_____

_____

_____

CREATIVE WORSHIP

"The Lord will guide you always; He will satisfy your needs in a sun-scorched land and will strengthen your frame. You will be like a well-watered garden, like a spring whose waters never fail."

Isaiah 58:11

26 NO MORE FEAR

Growing up I had a horrible fear of heights. It seemed any time I would walk up a flight of stairs, walk across a bridge, stand on a balcony, or near a mountain's edge, fear would grip my heart. My pulse would race and invariably it felt like something was pulling me down to the ground. It was one of the worst feelings ever.

As I think back, I wonder if my phobia began at our community pool. I remember one summer when I was still in elementary school having a traumatic experience on the high dive! As a child I absolutely LOVED to swim. In fact, my mom told me I would often jump out of the car and run to the pool leaving her screaming and chasing after me. She was sure I was going to jump into the water before she got my "bubble" (name for my life preserver) firmly secured around me! I guess it just never occurred to me there would be a reason to fear the water.

Until one terrifying day when I was convinced by some friends to jump from the high diving board.

I remember I started my climb with such excitement, but then about half way up, I happened to glance down. Gulp! I had never been that high before, and the excitement quickly drained from my little body. I slowly continued my climb and then took my first step out onto the diving board. Panic literally consumed me. I desperately tried to take a couple more steps but found myself completely frozen in fear. The sparkling oasis of fun that I had been splashing and playing in with my friends only moments before now looked SO far away!!!! I felt my stomach rise to my throat. I swallowed hard and whispered, "I can't do this!!"

I looked back at the ladder hoping for a quick escape only to be greeted with frustrated voices yelling, "Hurry up!" and "Jump, scaredy cat!" I'm sure I was only on that diving board for a few seconds, but it felt like an eternity. Sheepishly I carefully backed up and asked to retreat down the ladder. With great disdain I was allowed to make my way down to safety step by step, sharing a rung with each child that had patiently climbed to their "waiting place" in the line. It was simply HORRIBLE!

My fear of heights only intensified after that, and it would not be until I was in my twenties, leading a Christmas Production at my church, that I would face another terrifying climb that God actually used to set me free from this tormenting fear.

We had created a massive stage and at the very top, over 20' up in the air, a theatrical fabric (a scrim) needed to be hung. Unfortunately, not one volunteer showed up to help that night! (Of course they didn't!)

Knowing I HAD to do it, considering no one else was there, I started my climb as that ever-familiar pulling down sensation gripped every fiber of my being.

I remember praying the 91st Psalm, "Lord, you've given your angels charge over me…" I remember asking Holy Spirit to help me take my thoughts captive. I remember declaring Philippians 4:13, *"I can do all things through Christ who strengthens me."* I prayed in the Spirit, declared scripture, and worshiped without ceasing! It took me two hours to get that fabric hung, and they were the longest two hours of my life!

It actually wasn't until I was finishing that I realized I no longer was experiencing that "pulling down" sensation?! I don't know when it happened exactly, but somewhere in the midst of hanging that scrim, fear had left! With tears streaming down my face, I climbed down from that ladder and that 20' high assignment. I had been set free from my fear of heights. I had obeyed, trusted, and God had done a miracle!

Scripture References:

2 Timothy 1:7 "For God has not given us a spirit of fear, but of power and of love and of a sound mind." (NKJV)

2 Corinthians 10:5 "Casting down imaginations, and every high thing that exalteth itself against the knowledge of God, and bringing into captivity every thought to the obedience of Christ." (KJV)

Reflections:

1) What experiences have I had that have produced fear in me?

_____

_____

_____

_____

_____

_____

_____

2) What fear(s) do I need God to heal and take away from me?

_____

_____

_____

_____

_____

_____

_____

3) Are there any lies I'm believing that are preventing me from trusting God and experiencing His deliverance?

_____

_____

_____

_____

_____

_____

Prayer: Lord, You know the fears that lurk within my soul: ones I'm aware of and others that are hidden in the recesses of my mind. Would You search me and show me the root of those fears that I might release them to You? Your Word says You didn't give me a spirit of fear, but of power, love and a sound mind. Set me free from the lies that would keep me from believing this promise and prevent me from walking in the purposes and plans You have for me as Your child. Give me the faith of David that I may face my _giant of fear_, slay it, and remove it forever from my life. I trust You, Lord, and I'm ready to conquer this foe in Your authority and power. In Jesus Name.

Action Step(s)

_____

_____

_____

_____

_____

CREATIVE WORSHIP

"As for God, His way is perfect: The Lord's word is flawless;
He shields all who take refuge in Him."

Psalm 18:30

27 WE'RE ALL IN THIS TOGETHER

It was early morning: November 7, 2015. It was a day I had long been looking forward to: my daughter's first baby shower! However, instead of a day of celebration and dreams fulfilled, it quickly became my worst nightmare. That morning I received the most devastating news of my life, and in a matter of moments, I was launched into an emotional roller coaster ride like no other.

It would take everything I knew of God and His unwavering faithfulness to get me through that baby shower and ultimately that day. The day I had so looked forward to and now I could not wait for its end.

The following six days I walked through life like a zombie just going through the motions. I couldn't even find the strength to call on any of my friends; instead I allowed shock to catapult me into a cocoon of isolation. Then as if this wasn't enough, day seven came and so did another bout of bad news. My mom had fallen, and I needed to fly to Texas quickly. Still reeling from the bad news from the week prior, I made my plane reservation and headed home. Seven days later, my mom passed away. We planned a funeral, celebrated Thanksgiving, and buried my mom. Another week passed, and I was back on the ground at my job. I had lost three weeks and had a production to pull off, which required my writing, creating, rehearsing, and putting it on stage. Then, the week after was another series of shows. Everything was a blur, and I found myself functioning purely on autopilot and the amazing grace of God.

I wish I could say it ended there, but it did not. Every week for the next couple of months, I was hit with more and more distressing news. It felt like I was in a never-ending boxing match. A blow would come, and just as I would pull myself up, BAM! I would get hit yet again. It was worse than any nightmare I had ever experienced, and for the most part, I was walking it alone. At least for those first few weeks...

I'm going to stop here real quick and let you know that I'm not going to talk about the "bad news," but instead, I'm going to talk about the good news that I learned in walking through this season of my life.

First, no matter what ordeal or travesty is thrown at you during your lifetime, you NEVER have to walk through it alone. In Deuteronomy 31:8, we read that "...the Lord goes before you. He will be with you; He will not leave you or forsake you. Do not fear or be dismayed." This promise upheld me those first few devastating weeks. No longer was it simply a scripture written on a page, but it was now my reality! It had to be! Every excruciating moment, every painful discovery, and everything the enemy meant for evil, God was using it all to seal this promise on the pages of my heart never to be stripped away.

Second, I learned that inviting trusted friends into our struggles, while yielding to the Holy Spirit, allows heaven to touch earth. God never intended for us to walk through the trials of life alone, no matter how strong we think we are! In fact, He has given us brothers and sisters in Christ in order to help us through the often unforeseen and painful experiences we sometimes encounter in this life. The reality is that we live in a fallen world. Things, hard things, will happen! However, when we do life together, our load becomes lighter, and the embers of our hope can slowly be rekindled.

I'm now on the other side of this extremely painful season. And though I would not wish to walk this path again, I treasure what I have learned through the process. Jesus is faithful, and I can always trust Him to be with me no matter what life throws my way. He loves me without condition, and often loves me through the friends He has brought alongside me. That I don't have to do this thing called life alone. I've got Jesus, and I've got some pretty amazing friends! And so do you! He and Us. You and I! We're all in this together!

Scripture References:

Galatians 6:2 "Carry each other's burdens and in this way you will fulfill the law of Christ." (NIV)

Proverbs 17:17 "A friend loves at all times, and a brother is born for a time of adversity." (NIV)

Reflections:

1) What traumatic experiences do I need Jesus to "reframe" for me?

_____

_____

_____

_____

_____

_____

_____

_____

_____

2) Am I isolating when I should be in community? Why?

_____

_____

_____

_____

_____

_____

3) Who can I call upon to walk with me during this season of healing?

_____

_____

_____

_____

_____

Prayer: Father, You know the depth of my pain. You know how deeply it runs. I'm asking You to heal me and help me remember Your promise that You will always be with me and that You will never leave me nor forsake me. Help me step out of this fear and hopelessness and into Your hope and strength. Surround me with Your presence and bring trusted friends to support me during this season. Keep me from isolating or trying to do this on my own. Help me to trust You to work through those You place around me. Give them Your tenderness and wisdom to walk with me that we all might come to know You more intimately on this journey of restoration. I give You my heart and concerns right now and say, have Your way, Lord. In Jesus Name.

Action Step(s)

_____

_____

_____

_____

_____

CREATIVE WORSHIP

"One thing have I asked of the Lord, that will I seek after: that I may dwell in the house of the Lord all the days of my life, to gaze upon the beauty of the Lord and to inquire in his temple."

Psalm 27:4

28 SERVANTS OR CELEBRITIES

Back in the late 90's, I worked with a team of gifted artists to create an original production, "Overcoming the Dominion of Darkness." It was a full-length theatrical presentation that we would eventually take to Turkey three years in a row. Our final year included an unprecedented three-week tour, endorsed by the Turkish government, where we performed in the country's varying cultural centers.

What made it unprecedented was the government's signed documentation that opened doors for us to present a show embracing the biblical story of creation through the resurrection of Christ. This is not something that you would expect a Muslim nation of 70 million, with less than 1000 followers of Christ at the time, would want presented to their citizens. BUT God!

The first year we toured we found ourselves in a small amphitheater located in the center of Selcuk, biblical Ephesus. We had just completed our first show, and the cast was filtering out to greet the many waiting audience members. Desiring to make a connection with the people of Turkey, we had created postcards with our group picture, hoping to hand them out as gifts after our shows. Our small offering was greeted with many gracious smiles, head nods, and even a few warm hugs. It was the perfect icebreaker in the face of the obvious language barrier. What we didn't expect though, was shortly after the postcards had made their way out into the crowd, we began receiving requests for autographs. What?! Autographs?! But, we're not "celebrities!!"

The team was in shock. This was so unexpected! We were there to promote Jesus, not ourselves! I remember the team looking to me with questioning eyes and mouthing, "What do we do?" I mouthed back, "Sign the cards." At this point it would have brought more unnecessary attention to us had we *humbly* refused. We were there to build relationships and point people to Christ, and if signing a few autographs kept that door open, then we were going to do it!

In looking back, the experience easily could have opened the door to pride. Not that signing autographs in and of itself was wrong, but it definitely could have left room for us to think more highly of ourselves than we ought. As performing artists there is always the potential for pride to creep into our hearts and for our motives and identity to become twisted.

In fact, over the years I have found that most artists struggle with some level of insecurity and are either flying high on the applause and compliments of their audience or cowering in the valley of rejection because their performance was less than perfect, or they received some sort of critique. As Kingdom Artists it is so important that we guard our hearts and endeavor to stay God-centered instead of self-centered.

Honestly, shouldn't the goal of our art be to make the name of Jesus famous, not ours? I think John the Baptist said it best when he said of Jesus, *"He must become greater, and I must become less."* (John 3:30)

Does that mean we minimize our gifts and callings? Absolutely not! Proverbs 18:16 says, "A gift opens the way and ushers the giver into the presence of the great." God has given us gifts and talents to be used as platforms to glorify His name and as vehicles to bring the good news to our world.

That said, it isn't always easy to walk the path of a servant! But the rewards are eternal and will always be more gratifying than any celebrity status celebrated in this world. Yes, your flesh might have to die daily on this journey, but you can rest assured that in God's Kingdom, life ALWAYS springs forth from death. This is true for everyone, not just artists!

The question is, will we? Will we choose to gratify ourselves or instead use our gifts to worship God and minister the love of Christ to others? Will we make it about the message or the messenger? Will we choose to follow in Christ's footsteps who took on the nature of a servant? It's time to choose.

Scripture References:

Philippians 2:6-7 "Who, being in the very nature of God, did not consider equality with God something to be used to His own advantage; rather, He made Himself nothing by taking the very nature of a servant, being made in human likeness." (NIV)

Reflections:

1) Is my identity based on my *performance* and the approval of others?

_____

_____

_____

_____

_____

_____

_____

_____

2) Do I ever feel the need to name drop or "talk about my accomplishments," so that I feel valued in the eyes of others?

_____

_____

_____

_____

_____

_____

_____

3) How can I use my gifts and strengths to lift up Jesus' name instead of my own?

_____

_____

_____

_____

_____

_____

_____

Prayer: Lord, forgive me for the times when I've allowed insecurity and pride to lead me rather than You. Help me to embrace the gifts You have given me, not as a tool to make me feel better about myself, but as a vehicle to make Your name famous. Lord, would you use the gifts You've given me to open doors for me to share the gospel? And as I walk through those doors, may Your name become greater as I become less. I want to walk as You did, in the very nature of a servant. I ask You to anoint and empower me to do all that I have prayed. In Jesus Name.

Action Step(s)

_____

_____

_____

_____

_____

CREATIVE WORSHIP

"Sow righteousness for yourselves, reap the fruit of unfailing love, and break up your unplowed ground; for it is time to seek the Lord, until He comes and showers His righteousness on you."

Hosea 10:12

29 A CHRISTMAS GIFT

Christmas is one of my favorite times of year. I love everything about it! The twinkling lights, Christmas trees, beautiful songs, music, the ever-elusive snow, fun parties with family and friends, gift exchanges, AND the hours and hours of planning and rehearsing for Christmas productions!

For me there's just something so fulfilling about spending endless hours in rehearsals with a bunch of dancers, actors, aerialists, musicians, vocalists, techies, set designers, costumers, carpenters, painters, decorators...and don't forget the hospitality peeps! It just fills my soul to overflowing!

Years ago I remember working on one major Christmas production in particular. We had spent hours and hours planning, creating, and then implementing our dream. There were many nights that bled into mornings as we created sets, designed lighting, and rehearsed dance and theatre segments. I even remember falling asleep on pews a few nights!

As exhausting as the process was, I loved fanning the embers of my faith into flame as I leaned into Him for creativity and strength. The fruit of those hours of labor were never just a blessing for our audience, but they were used by God to draw me closer to Him and those that were on the journey with me.

The night of our last show one year, for some reason that I cannot remember at the moment, I had left my car in a nearby neighborhood close to a friend's home. I think we needed to pick up last minute items for the show and decided to ride together.

Regardless, we left my car and went to the church for our last performance. It went exceptionally well, and I can remember feeling so good about all that we had accomplished. The performers had given their all, and the audience had really appreciated the result. We finished the show, celebrated with the cast, and put everything away.

It was really late when we finally approached my friend's neighborhood. The plan was to pick up my car, head home, and drop into bed. We turned into the cul-de-sac, and there was no car. I thought that we are so tired that we had pulled onto the wrong street. A quick look around verified that we were in the right place, but where was my car?!?! I had to think back. This IS where I left my car, isn't it?!? Time seemed to stop as I tried to wrap my exhausted brain around the now-approaching reality that my car was gone. Stolen.

I couldn't believe it. I had just spent ALL these weeks and hours creating a show that would honor God and bless His people and our community! How could

He LET this happen? It just didn't seem fair. (I repented of this immature and wrong thinking the next day! As if!) Needless to say, the already late night got a LOT later. With police interviews, phone calls, and incident reports, it was a less-than-restful end to a very long day.

The next few days brought no good news. In fact, the police told me the car had most likely been disassembled and sold for parts, and I shouldn't plan on getting it back. It was disappointing and frustrating! I needed a car! However, by Christmas Eve, I was at peace. God had done so much work in my heart leading up to this; I just knew I could trust Him.

Christmas Eve came, and we spent the night with our dear friends, Kenny and Karen. I was not going to let the enemy steal my joy! We were going to celebrate and make lots of fun memories, which we did. It was a wonderful evening, and we woke up early Christmas morning to Karen's most delicious strawberry crepes. It was then, during breakfast, that I received a phone call from my in-laws. They told me, "Someone just dropped off an anonymous Christmas gift for you at our house, because you weren't home." I remember thinking, "How strange! Who could it have been? And what did they leave?"

A few hours later we pulled into my in-laws driveway to find someone had bought me a CAR and put it in my name! To say I was overwhelmed is an understatement. To this day I don't know who gave that car to me, but what I do know is that my Heavenly Father showed me once again, how very trustworthy He is, AND that He loves going above and beyond!

Scripture References:

Philippians 4:19 "And my God will meet all your needs according to the riches of His glory in Christ Jesus." (NIV)

Reflections:

1) Do I have any misplaced expectations that cause me to think God "owes" me?

_____

_____

_____

_____

_____

_____

2) Maybe I haven't received a car, but what has God provided for me? (Physically, spiritually, emotionally, relationally, financially)

_____

_____

_____

_____

_____

_____

3) Is God asking me to be His answer to someone else's need?

_____

_____

_____

_____

_____

Prayer: Lord, thank You that Your Word says that You will provide for my every need. I'm choosing to trust that promise, knowing You are fully aware of the areas where I lack. I believe You are already working on my behalf. As I wait upon You to do what only You can do, I want to make myself available to be a blessing to someone else. Give me eyes to see, ears to hear, and courage to step out in faith as You ask that of me. Cause my obedience to build someone else's faith even as You expand mine at the same time. In Jesus Name.

Action Step(s)

_____

_____

_____

_____

_____

_____

CREATIVE WORSHIP

"Jesus answered, 'I am the way and the truth and the life. No one comes to the Father except through Me.'"

John 14:6

30 MY VINDICATOR

Have you ever been misrepresented by someone? I have, and being someone who is very aware of my "witness," it was extremely painful.

In my early years of leading at the church, there was a woman upset by a new ministry I was starting. We had similar visions, and I thought I was creating something that would compliment her vision and cause it to expand and flourish. But instead of being excited by my *help*, she was deeply offended.

Once I realized I had created a problem, rather than a solution, I asked to meet with her. I wanted to reassure her of my intentions to encourage and support, not to compete nor take away! Everything I said was to no avail. She was angry, and nothing I said was going to change that. Soon after, unkind words and rumors began circulating about me. I was honestly both shocked and hurt.

Ultimately, this individual reached out to the church's Senior Leadership and asked to have a meeting with them and me. I remember sitting in my chair, surrounded by my pastors, listening to this person talk about me. I was accused of saying things I would never even think, much less say! It took everything within me not to interrupt and correct her words!

Finally, it got so bad I just couldn't be quiet any longer! Just as I was about to speak, I heard Holy Spirit say, "Be quiet." Unfortunately, a small sound did escape my mouth before I received this directive, so everyone was now staring at me. I waved them off and told them to continue. I completely disconnected from the conversation at that moment and began talking to God in my head! "But WHY?!? What she is saying is NOT true!! She is destroying my reputation! This is NOT ok!! I don't want my leadership thinking I would say the things she is suggesting!!" Once I stopped my ranting, I heard Holy Spirit whisper to me again, "Trust Me and just listen."

It was excruciating! As the conversation continued, my heart began to soften and I realized there were deep hurts at the root of her words. It was her truth, heard through a filter filled with pain from her past. As I listened, a supernatural compassion came over me, and by the meeting's end I actually prayed for her. It was nothing short of a miracle for me!

However, I was still struggling with the thought that my reputation had been "stolen" that day. I REALLY wanted to tell "my side of the story." I got a firm "NO" on that from Holy Spirit. So I offered the option of calling a few friends to tell them about "all I had endured." Got a FIRM "no," on that too. (It's actually funny now; then it was not). Throughout that evening I struggled as Holy Spirit continued to whisper, "Trust Me, I am your Vindicator." By morning, I had let it go and no longer had the *need* to "tell my side of the story," to anyone.

Later that day, I ventured into the church office and was greeted at the staff mailboxes by one of my Pastors. With an encouraging smile he said, "I want you to know that we all realize what was said yesterday was not fully the truth. In fact, that your ability to sit and listen, without defending yourself, said more than you could have ever said in your defense. We are grateful to have you as a part of our leadership team and trust you to handle the situation in whatever way you see is best."

What?!? My eyes totally teared up! God had vindicated me and without my *help*. Once again, God had proven His trustworthiness to me!

Since then I've had multiple times to apply this lesson. And truth be told, I don't always succeed at making the right choices. But when I do, it is ALWAYS so much better than when I try and take things into my own hands. (By the way, God graciously allowed me to be a part of the healing journey for the woman in this story.)

Scripture References:

Psalm 135:14 "For the Lord will vindicate His people and have compassion on His servants." (NIV)

Isaiah 54:17 "No weapon that is fashioned against you shall succeed, and you shall confute every tongue that rises against you in judgment. This is the heritage of the servants of the Lord and their vindication from Me, declares the Lord." (ESV)

Reflections:

1) Who do I need to forgive that has misrepresented me or my situation to others?

_____

_____

_____

_____

_____

_____

2) Write about a time when it would have been better to let God defend me rather than me defend myself.

_____

_____

_____

_____

_____

_____

3) What situation(s) am I facing that I need to entrust the outcome to God?

_____

_____

_____

_____

_____

Prayer: Father, first I want to acknowledge You know what is best for me! I will trust You to handle the concerns of my heart in the way You see is best. I will trust You as my vindicator, knowing You will not allow any weapon formed against me to prosper. You are compassionate and just. I will not react in fear or control but will rest in Your ability to refute any words wrongly spoken about me. I also ask You to examine my heart and correct me if my perspective is skewed or my words unkind. I give the outcome of my future to You, knowing You only want what is in my best interest. Let Your Kingdom come and Your will be done. In Jesus Name.

Action Step(s)

_____

_____

_____

_____

_____

CREATIVE WORSHIP

"For He will command His angels concerning you to guard you in all your ways."

Psalm 91:11

31 ANGELS AND JAZZ SHOES

I was co-leading a drama troupe and our team had been asked to do a New Year's Eve performance for a local church. Our performance would lead into a time of ministry scheduled for midnight. The church location was about an hour and a half away from where we were based. Being so far away, as well as it being a holiday, we were especially aware of the fact that we could not forget anything! There would be no time to "quickly run back home," should we forget something. With this in mind, we took extra care when loading all of the lighting, backdrops, costumes, and props. Everything had to be accounted for and was checked and rechecked multiple times.

Just before we pulled out, I ran upstairs to grab the last few things and do a final sweep of our apartment. As I was walking out the front door with my loaded arms, I saw my husband's jazz shoes sitting on the dining room table. They were a part of our troupe's uniform, and he definitely needed them. However, my hands were full, so as I exited I yelled out a quick reminder for him to grab them before locking up and heading down.

We were finally on our way so I pulled out a book I had been reading about Angels. The book told stories of these divine messengers being used by God to fulfill His purposes. There were biblical and modern-day examples, and I was enjoying cross referencing the scriptures as we drove along. Reading aloud much of what I was discovering, our discussion only sealed the truth of what I was seeing in scripture.

With my faith stirred, we arrived at the church where the rest of our team was waiting to help unload. There was a flurry of activity as we quickly started assembling everything and getting ready for the late evening performance. About an hour into our set up someone began laying out our costumes and noticed my husband's jazz shoes were missing. I immediately went and found him, asking if he had grabbed them from the dining room table before locking up the apartment. His response made me nervous. He couldn't remember if he had or not.

He quickly stopped what he was doing and ran out to the car to see if perhaps they had been left there. When he couldn't find them, I went and looked but didn't find them either. As a bit of panic began to overwhelm us, two more of our team members searched the car, just in case we had overlooked them. Nothing.

We were 3.5 hours from our show opening. That would give my husband just barely enough time to go home, grab his shoes, and arrive back in time for the show. Everyone was nervous about this prospect, concerned he might run into traffic delays with it being New Year's Eve. As we gathered to pray, I remembered the scriptures we had read on our drive over coming to mind. I thought, "Let's ask God to send His angels to bring us the jazz shoes!" And though I prayed for this in great faith, I really thought God would maybe send angels to escort him somewhere to FIND some jazz shoes, not actually get them for him. (Oh, when we try to figure out how God will answer our prayers!!)

We finished praying and my husband shot out the door, and we hurriedly resumed setting things up. It wasn't even five minutes later when my husband came walking back into the auditorium...holding his jazz shoes! We all looked on in disbelief. Where did you get those??? He said, "I got into the car and sitting on the back seat, all by themselves, were my shoes!"

Needless to say, our faith skyrocketed that night. By the end of our performance that evening, the presence of God was palpable. In fact, literally every person in the auditorium, with exception of one man, came forward for ministry and/or to receive Christ as Savior. God had sent His angels and fulfilled His will!!

Scripture References:

Hebrews 1:14 "Are not all angels ministering spirits sent to serve those who will inherit salvation?" (NIV)

Psalm 103:20 "Praise the Lord, you His angels, you mighty ones who do His bidding, who obey His word." (NIV)

Acts 5:19 "But during the night an angel of the Lord opened the doors of the jail and brought them out." (NIV)

Reflections:

1) In what area(s) does God want to expand my faith?

_____

_____

_____

_____

_____

_____

_____

2) What is hindering me from believing the promises in God's Word?

_____

_____

_____

_____

_____

_____

3) How can I expand my faith? What scriptures can I commit to memory?

_____

_____

_____

_____

_____

_____

Prayer: Father, thank You for sending Your angels to care for me and to assist with the fulfillment of Your will in my life. Help me to remember how You have sent Your angels to Your people in the past to open prison doors, close the mouths of lions, minister to the weary, and guard the steps of Your faithful ones to safety. Declaring Your word and contending with the devil on our behalf, I am grateful You have empowered them to assist me as I follow after You. You are such a good Father, always caring, guiding, and protecting me. Thank You for releasing Your angels, created to worship and serve You, to help me in times of need. In Jesus Name.

Action Step(s)

_____

_____

_____

_____

_____

CREATIVE WORSHIP

"From the rising of the sun to the place where it sets, the name of the Lord is to be praised."

Psalm 113:3

32 LOVE AND FORGIVENESS

When Jesus commanded us to love others, He didn't say that we had to agree with them first. Gulp, that can be SO hard!

What does love look like? Scripture tells us...

Love considers others first.
Love looks for the best.
Love shows respect.
Love seeks unity.
Love isn't selfish.
Love offers the best.
Love displays patience.

Loving others can involve pain. Love means giving of yourself. Love means putting your heart out there for someone to potentially wound you. Love means being selfless and thinking about the needs of others before we think of our own.

We'll never love someone without some discomfort accompanying that choice. It isn't easy, and sometimes it just feels unnatural, but loving others is something Jesus has called us to do as His followers.

He also has called us to forgive one another. This is another difficult command to follow.

If you're around people for more than minutes a day, you can be sure the opportunity to be offended will present itself. It may be something small or large; it may be intentional or not. The bottom line, when it arrives you will have a choice related to your response. Will you be quick to forgive? Or will you replay the scenario over and over again in your mind, allowing bitterness to take root in your heart?

The truth is, when we continually reflect on how wrong someone has acted toward us, even when we are "justified" in our stance, replaying scenarios over and over in our minds has the potential of creating walls within our hearts. These walls not only separate us from the people around us, but they also can separate us from displaying God's heavenly compassion. Beware! Bitterness is an ugly thing, and it is very dangerous.

God has given us a command to forgive, and it is for our good as much as it is for others. In fact, the fruit of unforgivenss is a life filled with oppression and destruction. Don't let the enemy twist that truth in your mind. You are not punishing the offender when you choose to hold on to a hurt. You are actually punishing yourself. Remember, forgiving the person who has offended, hurt, or mistreated you, does not excuse his or her behavior. What it does do is set YOU free!

So if I may gently encourage you: Stop replaying what happened over and over again in your mind, extend mercy over judgment, choose love over hate, and resolve to forgive your offender so that bitterness has no opportunity to take root in your heart! For Your own good, do it God's way! Let love prevail!

Scripture References:

John 13:34-35 "A new command I give you: Love one another. As I have loved you, so you must love one another. By this everyone will know that you are my disciples, if you love one another." (NIV)

Colossians 3:13 "Bear with each other and forgive one another if any of you has a grievance against someone. Forgive as the Lord forgave you." (NIV)

Luke 6:37 "Do not judge, and you will not be judged. Do not condemn, and you will not be condemned. Forgive, and you will be forgiven." (NIV)

Reflections:

1) Is it possible that my definition of love differs from God's? In what ways can I better "love" those around me?

_____

_____

_____

_____

_____

_____

_____

2) When I have failed, how has God shown His mercy, love, and forgiveness to me?

_____

_____

_____

_____

_____

_____

_____

3) Is there anyone I haven't REALLY forgiven? What do I need to stop replaying over and over in my mind?

_____

_____

_____

_____

_____

_____

_____

Prayer: Lord, help me love as You love. Help me to be quick to listen and slow to speak. And when I do speak, will You fill my mouth with Your words instead of my own? Help me to prefer others over myself, always looking for the best in each person I find before me. Let me be patient, slow to anger and quick to forgive. Let all that comes from my mouth be bathed in love, mercy and Truth. Cause me to be bold and courageous in my speech, yet filled with Your compassion, grace, and charity. Help me to always pursue unity, knowing where there is unity, there also is Your blessing. In Jesus Name.

Action Step(s)

_____

_____

_____

_____

_____

_____

_____

CREATIVE WORSHIP

"The Lord is my strength and my shield; my heart trusts in Him, and He helps me. My heart leaps for joy, and with my song I praise Him."

Psalm 28:7

33 TRUTH VS FEELINGS

As an "artist" and working with artists most of my life, it's true we can be pretty *emotional* beings. Honestly, our "sensitivity" is both our strength and our weakness. Being able to tap into our emotions, allows for the creation of some pretty beautiful, raw, deep, and genuine artistic expressions. On the other hand, those same emotions can be exhausting as the drama bleeds from the stage or canvas out into day-to-day living.

The fact is emotions are not very trustworthy and can sometimes lead us down a wrong pathway. However, I am so thankful God has given them to us.

When our emotions cooperate and are in agreement with the Truth, they are a beautiful thing. We feel the love of Jesus. We enjoy His majestic creation. We are moved in our hearts when we worship or hear a powerful message. All of these unique experiences are a gift to be treasured.

What's important to remember is: though God gave us emotions and as wonderful as they are, they were never intended to be our guide.

Our emotions are meant to respond to the Truth which is why it is so important that we fill our minds and hearts with God's Word.

I've come to realize over the years that I cannot even slightly trust my emotions when needing to make a decision. I must instead go to the truth of God's Word, and then call upon my emotions to agree with what Scripture says.

The same can be said about experiences. We cannot allow crises or bad experiences to color our thinking. Experiences and emotions, though often extremely convincing, cannot direct our footsteps. Both of them are untrustworthy. True discernment can only be found in Christ and His Word.

Proverbs 2 tells us to store up God's commands within us. It tells us to turn our ear to wisdom and to apply our hearts to understanding. It also says that if we call out for insight and if we search for it (in God's Word) as if we were searching for a hidden treasure, God will give us knowledge and understanding.

It is in gaining Godly wisdom and understanding that we will be able to embrace the joy of our emotions rather than becoming slaves to them.

How often have I made decisions based on a fleeting feeling that by day's end had changed. Too many times my misguided choices have led me down a path that was less than wonderful and sometimes irreversible. This can be devastating, and often it could have been easily avoided had I allowed the Word of God to direct me rather than a feeling.

So as we approach the things of life, may I encourage you to seek God's truth, wisdom, knowledge and understanding before making any choices about ANYthing! And should your emotions attempt to take the lead, quickly and sharply bring them into submission. It is here, alone, that you will find the success and protection needed to walk through this life!

Scripture References:

Proverbs 2:1-11 "My son, if you accept My words and store up My commands within you, turning your ear to wisdom and applying your heart to understanding—indeed, if you call out for insight and cry aloud for understanding, and if you look for it as for silver and search for it as for hidden treasure, then you will understand the fear of the Lord and find the knowledge of God. For the Lord gives wisdom; from His mouth come knowledge and understanding. He holds success in store for the upright,He is a shield to those whose walk is blameless, for He guards the course of the just and protects the way of His faithful ones. Then you will understand what is right and just and fair—every good path. For wisdom will enter your heart, and knowledge will be pleasant to your soul. Discretion will protect you, and understanding will guard you." (NIV)

Reflections:

1) Do I allow emotions to direct my decisions? List some examples.

_____

_____

_____

_____

_____

_____

_____

2) What have the results been when I've allowed my feelings to direct my choices rather than wisdom?

_____

_____

_____

_____

_____

_____

_____

3) When I feel strongly about something, what steps should I take before taking action?

_____

_____

_____

_____

_____

_____

Prayer: Lord, I'm grateful for the sensitivity that You've placed within the secret places of my heart. I am grateful for the many experiences that have brought me so much joy. I'm thankful for the times I've felt Your love and closeness during worship and when my heart has leapt as the power of Your Word penetrated my soul! At the same time, I ask for Your forgiveness for the times I've allowed my emotions to rule me instead of Scripture. I ask You, Lord, to help me bring my feelings into agreement with Your Word, that my walk might be blameless and that I might rest in the fullness of Your protection. In Jesus Name.

Action Step(s)

_____

_____

_____

_____

_____

_____

CREATIVE WORSHIP

"But the fruit of the Spirit is love, joy, peace, forbearance, kindness, goodness, faithfulness, gentleness and self-control."

Galatians 5:22-23

34 AN OPPORTUNITY TO SERVE

When the Covid pandemic hit, there was so much uncertainty and fear. I can remember at the very beginning people were frightened to even go to the grocery store. And if they actually made it to the store, most found the shelves were empty. It was simply surreal.

About two weeks into the pandemic, I was at a grocery store near my home, and the woman checking me out told me they were struggling finding people to work. Everyone was sequestering themselves at home and didn't want to put themselves in harm's way. She elaborated saying it looked like they were going to have to limit their hours of operation, which she was concerned would negatively impact some of their elderly customers. As I listened to her talk, this great sense of empathy overwhelmed me. And it didn't dissipate as I drove home; it only intensified.

You see, all through high school and college I had worked in grocery stores. I was a checker, a stocker, and quickly moved into management. I had pretty much worked every area - except with the butcher (ick). As I reflected, knowing high school and college were both MANY years ago, I still thought, "Surely there is something I can do to help."

The next day I decided to put in a few applications to some local grocery stores. Surprisingly, I actually heard back from Walmart within an hour of submitting my resume. The manager called me and hired me on the spot. They desperately needed "shoppers" to fill orders for the many vulnerable and elderly people frightened to come in and shop for themselves. I thought, "This is exactly who I want to help!" I accepted the position and started the following week.

It was long hours, and I quickly realized this wasn't going to be as easy as I had thought! About three weeks in, I was out on the floor filling one of my many orders. My feet hurt, my body was aching, and I was just overall tired. I was struggling and had to keep asking God to keep reminding me "why" I decided to do this! I didn't necessarily need the money, so I could easily just walk away.

At that moment, I had to discipline my thoughts! I can remember telling myself, "This minor discomfort you are experiencing is NOTHING compared to what Jesus endured on your behalf. Stop this! He stepped down from glory, clothed Himself in flesh, was scourged and beaten, and died on a cross. He served you with His life! Get over yourself." (I honestly have to do a lot of self-talk, or I can quickly succumb to self-pity.)

As I was self-coaching and pulling my next items from the shelf, an elderly gentleman approached me asking for help. Fortunately, I knew where to find what he needed, and we quickly had it in his cart! All was well! As I turned to go back to my personal shopper duties, he reached out to me and said, "I just wanted to thank you for all your hard work and for being here so we can get the things we need. I'm so grateful for your sacrifice and I wanted you to know just how much it means to me and my wife."

I totally teared up. THIS! This was why I had taken the job. This was why I was going to press through my discomfort. This was why I was here! I could not have been more grateful in that moment for God's gracious reminder.

Since then, I've often reflected on how easy it is to start with the right intentions only to find yourself off track because your eyes moved from the finish line (your why) to you! I will never forget this special season in my life. I'm so very thankful that the Lord gave me this small opportunity to die to myself and serve my community.

Scripture References:

Proverbs 3:27 "Do not withhold good from those to whom it is due, when it is in your power to act." (NIV)

Galatians 6:2 "Bear one another's burdens, and so fulfill the law of Christ." (ESV)

I Peter 4:10 "As each has received a gift, use it to serve one another, as good stewards of God's varied Grace." (ESV)

Reflections:

1) When have I lost sight of my "why?"

_____

_____

_____

_____

_____

_____

_____

_____

_____

2) Do I sometimes struggle with self-pity? How can I change that?

_____

_____

_____

_____

_____

_____

3) Is there something I'm avoiding that I could be doing to help someone else?

_____

_____

_____

_____

_____

_____

Prayer: Father, I ask You to give me Your heart of compassion and empathy. Help me to see where there are needs and where my gifts could be used to serve someone else. Help me to place my eyes on You that Your example of servanthood might direct my choices. And when challenges arise and the assignment You give me becomes difficult, keep me from moving my attention to myself and operating in self-pity. I ask You to open doors of opportunity for me to serve, carry the burdens of others, and love people as Christ loved me with His life. In Jesus Name.

Action Step(s)

_____

_____

_____

_____

_____

_____

CREATIVE WORSHIP

*"Enter His gates with thanksgiving and His courts with praise;
give thanks to Him and praise His name."*

Psalm 100:4

35 KEEP KNOCKING

Back in the early 2000s, I was studying and really seeking God about unity in the Body of Christ. During this time, I wrote a show called MOSAIC. To say it was a "unique" production might be an understatement. Think Cirque du Soleil with a strong biblical message on a fraction of the budget!

Encompassing original music, a crazy set, dance, theatre, illusions, and some pretty cool lighting and technology, it was an exciting and huge endeavor! It was one that built my faith and the faith of many others who joined me on the journey. The show was successful on many levels and ran for a couple of weeks before we closed and had to put everything away.

As I sat at my desk a few weeks after the show closed, I realized we still had $500 left in unpaid bills. I remember looking at those ominous invoices laying on my desk and thinking, "I have no idea how I'm going to pay these!" I had scraped together every penny I could to produce the show, and there was nothing in my savings account to "save-the-day." My only backup plan was Jesus! (This is the best backup plan by the way, but also one that rarely unfolds the way you envision it!)

I looked again, with a bit of trepidation at the bills laying on my desk. Then, I said a prayer that went something like this: "Lord, I know you told me to produce this show. I did my best to steward every penny we received. I have no money left to pay these bills. We must pay them, Lord, lest people think *we* are irresponsible and untrustworthy. That would be a horrible witness, Lord. What are You going to do about this? *Your* reputation is on the line!" (I somewhat laugh at this prayer now, but it was where I was in my journey, and believe it or not, I was sincerely concerned about *our* witness!)

It was Christmas time, and the bills were due in January. I had plans to spend the holidays at my sister's home, and so I left with no answer to my dilemma. EVERY day while I was at my sister's, I "reminded" the Lord about the bills that needed to be paid. Then, one morning as I was *reminding* Him yet again, I heard these words in my mind. "You don't need to remind Me about that anymore." I thought, "Was that You, Lord?" Then I wondered if perhaps my prayers were annoying Him. I stopped praying about those bills that day and instead chose to just trust and worship Him.

A week later I returned home and to my office. I wasn't looking forward to dealing with those unpaid invoices! On the way to my desk, I stopped by my office mailbox and picked up the stack of mail that currently filled it to overflowing.

While thumbing through everything, I noticed the address on one envelope was handwritten, so I pulled it out first. As I opened it, I quickly saw there was a check wrapped in a white piece of paper with a short note. It said, "As I was praying, the Lord told me to send this to you. God Bless." It was a check for $500 from someone I hadn't spoken to in years! Overwhelmed with tears, I picked up the envelope again and looked at its postmark. It was the day I had heard the Lord say to me, "You don't have to remind Me about that anymore." I don't think God was annoyed with me that day. He had just paid the bills…as only He can!

Scripture References:

Luke 11:5-10 "Then, teaching them more about prayer, He used this story: "Suppose you went to a friend's house at midnight, wanting to borrow three loaves of bread. You say to him, 'A friend of mine has just arrived for a visit, and I have nothing for him to eat.' And suppose he calls out from his bedroom, 'Don't bother me. The door is locked for the night, and my family and I are all in bed. I can't help you.' But I tell you this—though he won't do it for friendship's sake, if you keep knocking long enough, he will get up and give you whatever you need because of your shameless persistence. "And so I tell you, keep on asking, and you will receive what you ask for. Keep on seeking, and you will find. Keep on knocking, and the door will be opened to you. For everyone who asks, receives. Everyone who seeks, finds. And to everyone who knocks, the door will be opened." (NLT)

Reflections:

1) About what have I stopped praying, because I've given up?

_____

_____

_____

_____

_____

_____

_____

2) What do I need to recommit to prayer?

_____

_____

_____

_____

_____

_____

_____

3) What scriptures and promises of God can I stand on related to my need(s)?

_____

_____

_____

_____

_____

_____

_____

Prayer: Lord, Your Word says You know our needs before we even ask. You tell us to not worry but to instead seek Your Kingdom and righteousness. Your promise is that when we do these things, You will provide for our needs, even as You do for the birds of the air and the lilies of the field. Today I bring my concerns and needs to You, trusting that as I ask, I will receive. As I seek, I will find. As I knock, the door will be opened. There is no need I have that is greater than Your provision. I ask You to do what only You can do, Lord. Glory and Honor to You. In Jesus Name.

Action Step(s)

_____

_____

_____

_____

_____

_____

_____

CREATIVE WORSHIP

"*He lifted me out of the slimy pit, out of the mud and mire; He set my feet on a rock and gave me a firm place to stand.*"

Psalm 40:2

36 HIS THRONE DESCENDED

We were nearing the end of our two-week tour in Turkey. When I say tour, we had taken a theatrical production of God's story, creation through the resurrection of Jesus, to a nation of over 70 million people with less than 1000 followers of Christ.

This was only one of three tours we would eventually take and each of them was filled with miraculous encounters and faith-building experiences. These trips and how I came to know God more intimately through them will forever reside within my heart.

Our first year we did not have one performance scheduled. We landed in the country, and then God opened doors for us one-by-one! Every show He divinely put in place as we followed Him day by day. It was like nothing I had ever experienced.

Our last stop on this particular tour was in the town of Dikili. We had hoped to perform here but initially met with nothing but closed doors. With only one night left before our departure back to the States, the hotel in which we were staying invited us to perform on the large patio area surrounding their pool. God had once again opened a door of opportunity! We knew it was going to be a late night, and we had to be at the airport EARLY the following day, but everyone agreed that we wouldn't sleep. We needed to share the Good News with the people of Dikili!

We spent the afternoon blocking and preparing for the performance now scheduled for that evening. Simultaneously, word of our upcoming show was being circulated around the town. By evening, using our tour bus to bring people to the hotel, we had a nice crowd seated and ready for our show to begin.

As we prepared to take the "stage," we gathered behind our show's backdrop for prayer. It was during this time that I had a vision of what appeared to be God on His throne, surrounded by myriads of angels, descending into the heart of what was about to happen. He had come to receive our worship, and His presence was tangible as we began the performance.

By the show's end it was obvious God had touched the hearts of those in attendance. For most it was their first time to hear the story of Christ and His redemptive love. As we circulated amongst the people, we soon discovered the town's mayor was in attendance. He loved the show and asked if we would return and perform it at their town's festival the following year. A government official in a Muslim nation wanted to feature our show about Christ at their town festival!! This incredible invitation was actually a foreshadowing of what was to come in the following years when we would receive permission from Turkey's national government to perform our show in their cultural centers!

The presence of God moved the hearts of men that night and opened doors that only He could open. Most assuredly God is enthroned in the praises of His people and will make His name known!

Scripture References:

Psalm 22:3 "But You are holy, O You who are enthroned in [the holy place where] the praises of Israel [are offered]." (Amplified)

I Chronicles 16:23-28 "Sing to the Lord, all the earth; proclaim His salvation day after day. Declare His glory among the nations, His marvelous deeds among all peoples. For great is the Lord and most worthy of praise; He is to be feared above all gods. For all the gods of the nations are idols, but the Lord made the heavens. Splendor and majesty are before Him; strength and joy are in His dwelling place. Ascribe to the Lord, all you families of nations, ascribe to the Lord glory and strength." (NIV)

Psalm 99:1-3 "The Lord reigns, let the nations tremble; He sits enthroned between the cherubim, let the earth shake. Great is the Lord in Zion; He is exalted over all the nations. Let them praise Your great and awesome name— He is Holy." (NIV)

Reflections:

1) In what areas of my life do I need to step out in faith?

_____

_____

_____

_____

_____

_____

_____

_____

_____

_____

_____

2) What am I reading, listening to or watching that I need to replace with Scripture and worship music? How might this help build my faith and trust in God?

_____

_____

_____

_____

_____

_____

_____

3) Is there anything or anyone I'm putting in front of my time with God that needs to be removed or placed further down on my list of priorities?

_____

_____

_____

_____

_____

_____

Prayer: Lord, I exalt Your name and give You all my praise. I place You above every person, thing, and dream I have. You are the source of my life, my salvation, my joy, and my peace. You alone are my everything. Forgive me when I have lost sight of this and looked for fulfillment in people, things, and experiences. I invite You to stir my faith and challenge me to trust You more in the things that so easily bring worry and fear into my life. Today I'm choosing prayer and worship as my weapons against all that would try to defeat me. In Jesus Name.

Action Step(s)

_____

_____

_____

_____

CREATIVE WORSHIP

"Every valley shall be raised up, every mountain and hill made low;
the rough ground shall become level, the rugged places a plain."

Isaiah 40:4

37 GUARD YOUR HEART

For years I was the Creative Pastor for our church and spent a lot of time in the "backstage" area during the week.

One day I was walking through the Music Room and ran into a friend. We stopped to chat for a moment when she began relaying an unfortunate story about someone we both knew. I honestly can't remember what it was all about, but I remember it was not a good report.

As she continued sharing the less-than-savory story, I felt myself getting drawn deeper and deeper into the conversation. In fact, I specifically remember starting to take a step closer as I didn't want to miss any details. I literally had a vision in my mind of a snare on the floor in front of me. A snare is a trap for catching birds or animals and typically one having a noose of wire or cord. The image in my mind was so vivid that I literally took a step back to avoid being caught in it.

I heard Holy Spirit whisper, "This conversation is a trap." I looked up at the girl who was telling me the story and said, "We cannot continue this conversation. It is not helpful, and I actually believe the enemy is using it to draw us into some sort of trap. Please don't tell me any more details."

Fortunately, she was not offended but instead agreed the discussion should stop. Instead of talking, we stood there together and prayed. We repented for allowing the conversation to go on as long as it had, and then we prayed for the individual and her situation.

I have to confess that I have not always responded this well when entering into a "concerned" discussion about someone else. Too often, I have either felt justified to give a bit more information or listen to a few more details so that I might pray more "effectively."

The reality is God is fully aware of every detail in every situation. If He wants us to be "more-in-the-know," I have found that Holy Spirit is perfectly capable of revealing and guiding us as specifically as needed during our prayer time.

As we mature in Christ, it is so important to keep a guard over our mouths, to refrain from unwholesome talk and to only speak those things that are helpful in building others up.

Does this mean we don't address things that need to be addressed? Of course not! God has given us scripture for teaching, reproof, correction, and for training in righteousness. God wants us free, complete, and equipped for every good work.

If you're ever unsure about "sharing" something, consider the following: Are you genuinely concerned for the welfare of the individual? Can the person with whom you're sharing actually make a difference in the situation? By not sharing, are you potentially putting this individual or the people around him or her in harm's way? Though this is definitely not an exhaustive list, it is certainly a starting point.

Scripture References:

Psalm 141:3 "Set a guard over my mouth, Lord; keep watch over the door of my lips." (NIV)

Ephesians 4:29 "Do not let any unwholesome talk come out of your mouths, but only what is helpful for building others up according to their needs, that it may benefit those who listen." (NIV)

James 1:26 "Those who consider themselves religious and yet do not keep a tight rein on their tongues deceive themselves, and their religion is worthless." (NIV)

Proverbs 18:7 "The mouths of fools are their undoing, and their lips are a snare to their very lives." (NIV)

2 Timothy 3:16-17 "All Scripture is breathed out by God and profitable for teaching, for reproof, for correction, and for training in righteousness, that the man of God may be complete, equipped for every good work." (ESV)

Reflections:

1) In what conversations have I engaged that were not necessary?

_____

_____

_____

_____

_____

_____

_____

_____

2) When I'm speaking both to and about someone, how can I guard my mouth and ensure the words I speak honor God and others?

_____

_____

_____

_____

_____

_____

_____

3) Are there any conversations I have avoided because of fear, insecurities, or uncertainty that need to happen?

_____

_____

_____

_____

_____

_____

Prayer: Lord, I ask You to set a guard over my mouth and keep watch over the door of my lips. Keep unwholesome talk far from my speech and help me foresee any snares the enemy might set before me. Help me to discern my motives before I share any concern I have about someone else or their situation. And will You give me the courage to speak up whenever it is truly necessary? May my words always be bathed in love, coated in mercy, and extended with grace. In Jesus Name.

Action Step(s)

_____

_____

_____

_____

_____

CREATIVE WORSHIP

"We don't yet see things clearly. We're squinting in a fog, peering through a mist. But it won't be long before the weather clears and the sun shines bright! We'll see it all then, see it all as clearly as God sees us, knowing Him directly just as He knows us!"

1 Corinthians 13:12

38 HEAR MY BATTLE CRY

Receiving the message from my doctor that there were some concerns about my mammogram and that I needed to go in for a biopsy was the last thing I wanted to hear that day. Though it would take a few more weeks, that biopsy would eventually reveal that I had stage 2 breast cancer.

It may be strange to say this, but I never really had any fear related to that diagnosis. I think my family and some of my friends might have been more traumatized by the news than I. For me it was about the potential inconvenience and interruption in my plans!

You see, the year before this diagnosis my world had been completely turned upside down. Everything I thought I knew about my life was in fact, not the reality I was living. That year had been one filled with shock, disbelief, pain, depression, hopelessness, mistrust, and the most devastating of heartaches. But God never left my side through it all! In fact, my faith and trust in Him grew by leaps and bounds during that time. I knew He would walk with me through this challenge as well.

Before receiving the news that I had breast cancer, I had scheduled a weekend in the Shenandoah mountains for some personal ministry with Pastors Bill and Sylvie Suddeth. After all I had walked through the year before, I had hoped this time would help me close a chapter and begin a new one. I would have never guessed that God had so much more in mind when guiding me to plan this trip.

We were finishing up our three days of ministry together when Pastor Bill opened his Bible to read a scripture to me. As he did, a cough drop wrapper fell from the pages. I remember him picking it up and saying, "This is so strange. I don't remember putting this in here." Looking up at me, he continued, "I actually just went through my Bible last week and cleaned everything out." He looked back at the wrapper and read it aloud, "'Let's hear your battle cry.'" As he handed it to me, he said, 'I can't help but believe this is from God for you." I took the wrapper from him and placed it in my journal, not realizing it would be the first of three *words* of encouragement God would send to *arm* me for my battle with cancer.

About a week after returning home from my mini-retreat, I received a Facebook message from a young woman involved in our women's ministry at church. She had sent me a devotional from one of Max Lucado's books. It was about David and Goliath. As I was reading, there was a phrase that referenced David's "battle cry." It jumped off the page at me as I was reminded of the cough drop wrapper stored safely in my journal. My faith was stirred! Then a few days later I was carrying an armload of things into the church when I noticed a wadded piece of paper on the sidewalk outside the entrance. Balancing what I was holding, I reached down to pick it up so that I could throw it away when I got to my office.

Dropping everything on my desk, I reached over to grab the "trash" I had just recovered so I could throw it away. However, when I did, for some reason the texture of the paper caught my attention. Instead of dropping it into the trash, I opened it up and smoothed it out only to find it was actually a page torn from a Bible. As I looked at it more closely, I saw the page was taken from the book of I Samuel, the story of David and Goliath! I heard the Spirit of God whisper to me, "Let's hear your battle cry." I knew then, without a shadow of doubt, that this battle belonged to the Lord. I had no need to fear!

There is nothing like doing life with Jesus. His perfect love will always cast out all fear, especially when you have to face giants!

Scripture References:

I Samuel 17:45-47 "David said to the Philistine, 'You come against me with sword and spear and javelin, but I come against you in the name of the Lord Almighty, the God of the armies of Israel, whom you have defied. This day the Lord will deliver you into my hands, and I'll strike you down and cut off your head. This very day I will give the carcasses of the Philistine army to the birds and the wild animals, and the whole world will know that there is a God in Israel. All those gathered here will know that it is not by sword or spear that the Lord saves; for the battle is the Lord's, and He will give all of you into our hands.'" (NIV)

Reflections:

1) What giants am I facing that are trying to bring fear into my life?

_____

_____

_____

_____

_____

_____

_____

_____

2) Am I looking to people or things, rather than God, to overcome any of my giants?

_____

_____

_____

_____

_____

_____

_____

3) What weapons has God placed in my hand to defeat the giants I'm currently facing? List those scriptures below.

_____

_____

_____

_____

_____

_____

Prayer: Lord, You know the giants I'm facing in my life right now. I ask You to enable me to see each of them through Your eyes, that I not be overcome by fear. I know You have given me the exact weapons I need to defeat my every foe. Stir my faith and make me strong and courageous as my battle cry of trust in You breaks forth. Deliver every giant into my hands, as I entrust my every battle to You. I am more than a conqueror in Christ, and I will overcome by the blood of the Lamb. In Jesus Name.

Action Step(s)

_____

_____

_____

_____

_____

_____

CREATIVE WORSHIP

"May the God of hope fill you with all joy and peace as you trust in Him, so that you may overflow with hope by the power of the Holy Spirit."

Romans 15:13

39 IF YOU'RE REALLY GOD

"I'm at the end of my rope!" "I can't take this anymore!" "I just want the pain to go away!" That's exactly where I was a little over 35 years ago. Although I had been raised in a Christian home and attended a church during my childhood and teenage years, something was missing.

Things had really started getting off track when I left home for a nearby State University. My newfound freedom as a college student soon distanced me from not only my home, but also my Christian upbringing. I was now in the party scene and on a path set for destruction.

One bad choice led to another, and I ended up leaving my dance scholarship and state title to follow my boyfriend to Dallas. An unhealthy relationship, coupled with drug use, soon led to a necessary escape to Arizona. My dreams and world had fallen apart, and I felt like a complete failure.

Those first months after arriving in Arizona, overwhelmed and feeling lost, I became suicidal. But in the midst of my heartache, God began sending laborers across my path. Many gave me random slips of paper with scriptures on them. Though initially I was annoyed, curiosity soon got the better of me, and I was digging into my still-packed boxes to retrieve my old childhood Bible. I just had to know what those scriptures said!

I remember one evening speaking to my mom on the phone. I told her I was depressed, I didn't know anyone, I didn't have friends, and I hated the desert! I didn't share about feeling suicidal, but I did mention that I had pulled out my Bible to look up a scripture someone had given me. THIS was her door of opportunity – through which she quickly jumped! She began encouraging me to get out the Yellow Pages. (Does anyone remember those??) She wanted me to see if I could find a nice church to attend and perhaps a local theatre. "You've always enjoyed drama, and I'm sure you could make some new friends there…" Not enjoying the turn in our conversation, I told her I would think about it, and I quickly ended the phone call.

As I got ready for bed that night, I decided I would try that "prayer thing" one more time. I basically told God, "If you're real and not just some story book character, then You can find me the church and theatre where I can meet some friends." (Disclaimer: There may have been a few expletives integrated into this prayer. I was in a pretty dark place in my life.) The next day I came home early from work, and a few moments after arriving, there was a knock at the door. It was a guy from the Mayflower moving company. He had a delivery for a house down the street, but no one was home. He asked to use my phone to call his dispatch office. (This was before mobile phones, if you can imagine.) I told him

"Sure," and he came in and used the phone. When he completed his call, we continued to talk which allowed him to notice my then thick Texas accent.

He asked me how long I had been in Arizona and if I had found a church. And if I had not, he asked if I would like to join him at his. At this point, I didn't give a thought to my prayer from the night before. I just thought, "He's cute. Sure I'll go to church with him." We chatted a bit longer and then agreed we would go together the following weekend. Then as he opened the door to leave, he stopped abruptly and turned around to face me. I almost ran into him! He said, "I don't know if you're interested in drama or not, but I'm a member of a theatre troupe at my church that meets on Wednesdays, and if you want, I could take you to that, too." It was at this moment that I suddenly remembered my prayer from the night before: "If you're really God, then you can find me a church and a theatre group." I remember a shiver going up my spine as I told him "ok" and bid him a quick goodbye. I'm not going to lie. I was pretty freaked out in that moment! Did that really just happen?!

My prayer had been coarse and my heart hard, but God loved and pursued me anyway. He even sent someone directly to my front door! The next week I went to church with that young man and gave my life to Christ. A broken life, a desperate prayer, and an obedient servant of Christ forever changed the trajectory of my life. I was never the same again.

Scripture References:

Ezekiel 34:16 "I will seek the lost, bring back the scattered, bind up the broken and strengthen the sick…" (NASB)

Reflections:

1) Do I need to stop running from God in any area of my life?

_____

_____

_____

_____

_____

_____

_____

_____

_____

2) In what areas of my life do I need God's intervention?

_____

_____

_____

_____

_____

_____

3) Is God asking me to reach out to anyone around me with His love and Truth?

_____

_____

_____

_____

_____

_____

Prayer: Father, I thank You so much for loving me exactly where I am, while also loving me enough to not leave me there! Thank You that no matter how far I might wander, You will always come after me. I ask You to seal Your love for me in my heart. Uncover any lies the enemy might speak to me that would distort that unconditional love and keep me from the plans You have to prosper me, to keep me from harm, and to give me hope and a future. Forewarn me of the snares the enemy might set before me while also giving me a heart that extends beyond myself and to the welfare of others. I make myself available, as an instrument in Your hand, to point others to You. Use me, Lord, for Your Kingdom purposes. In Jesus Name.

Action Step(s)

_____

_____

_____

_____

_____

CREATIVE WORSHIP

"*As water reflects a face, so a man's heart reflects the man.*"

Proverbs 27:19

40 THEY WILL KNOW US BY OUR LOVE

We had been touring shows through the country of Turkey for almost two weeks. We had just done a show the night before, and we had one last one to perform before heading home the following day. Needless to say, we were a bit weary and in much need of a rejuvenating break.

That afternoon we were provided with a few hours of down time, so a bunch of us headed to the pool to enjoy some refreshing and relaxing time in the water. Though we had spent hours together on a bus over the last two weeks, loaded and unloaded that same bus multiple times as we moved across the country changing hotels and performing in different cities, we fortunately still loved each other and actually enjoyed hanging out together!

It was a beautiful sunny day, and everyone was having fun laughing and playing silly games. There was nothing out of the ordinary: just swimming and a little game of Marco Polo.

It was during this time of splashing around that a Russian woman staying at our hotel approached a couple of our ministry team members. In broken English she shared some of her past and the unfortunate encounters she had experienced in her country with those that professed to be Christians. In fact, she had rejected Christ and the Christian religion based on these hurtful and controlling encounters. (Unfortunately, this is not the first time I've heard stories like this, and it always breaks my heart.)

As she continued, her countenance suddenly changed as she went on to tell how much she had enjoyed our show from the previous night. She loved "our" Jesus. He was "different" than the one to whom she had been introduced in her country.

It was both obvious and amazing how God had touched her during the performance. But more than that, as she continued sharing, we found out what really impacted her was the way our team treated one another, the hotel staff, and her! She said she had been watching us, and we were "different," too. We were like the Jesus in our story.

She told our team that she was leaving that day and would not be there for our last performance, but she wanted us to know that she had changed her mind about Jesus. She now wanted to be one of His followers.

What an incredible reminder of the impact our words and actions can have on others. It reminds me of the quote by St Francis of Assisi, "Preach the Gospel at all times; when necessary, use words."

This beautiful moment forever resides in my heart as a reminder of how my actions can speak more loudly than my words. May I never forget the gift, nor the responsibility, I have been given as a follower of Jesus Christ. I am to love others as He has loved us, and never forget that people are watching.

Scripture References:

John 13:34-35 "A new command I give you: Love one another. As I have loved you, so you must love one another. By this everyone will know that you are my disciples, if you love one another." (NIV)

Acts 1:8 "But you will receive power when the Holy Spirit comes on you; and you will be my witnesses in Jerusalem, and in all Judea and Samaria, and to the ends of the earth." (NIV)

I Peter 2:11-12 "Dear friends, I urge you, as foreigners and exiles, to abstain from sinful desires, which wage war against your soul. Live such good lives among the pagans that, though they accuse you of doing wrong, they may see your good deeds and glorify God on the day He visits us." (NIV)

Matthew 5:16 "In the same way, let your light shine before others, that they may see your good deeds and glorify your Father in heaven." (NIV)

John 3:17 "For God did not send His Son into the world to condemn the world, but in order that the world might be saved through Him." (ESV)

Reflections:

1) Is there anything in my words, actions, or attitudes that might be misrepresenting Christ?

_____
_____
_____
_____
_____
_____
_____
_____
_____
_____

2) In what way(s), does my life point others to Christ?

_____

_____

_____

_____

_____

_____

_____

3) What things might need to change in me in order for others to see Jesus more clearly?

_____

_____

_____

_____

_____

_____

_____

Prayer: Lord, thank You for the opportunity You give us as Your children to be a part of Your plans in this world: plans to bring others into Your loving and saving grace. I ask that You would supernaturally help me to lay down my selfish and sinful desires that would cause others to stumble. Instead cause me to hunger after the things that would bring glory to Your name. I want Your light to shine through me, I want to be a reflection of Your goodness, and I want my life to be used for Your Kingdom purposes. Lord, I give you my life to mold and shape as only You can. In Jesus name.

Action Step(s)

_____

_____

_____

_____

_____

CREATIVE WORSHIP

"Peace I leave with you; My peace I give you. I do not give to you as the world gives. Do not let your hearts be troubled and do not be afraid."

Romans 15:13

BECOMING A CHRIST FOLLOWER

If you have not already made the decision to follow Christ, I would love to tell you more about the beautiful gift God has provided for you in Jesus and invite you to join me on this amazing journey as a Christ Follower.

A few things you should know:

1) We ALL are sinners and will rightly stand under the judgment of God.

2) God loves us, and Jesus came to earth to make forgiveness and salvation possible. Jesus died on the cross as the complete sacrifice for our sins. He took upon Himself the judgment we deserve.

3) God in His incredible grace offers us the gift of eternal life. But like any gift, it only becomes ours when we respond and receive it.

4) Salvation is intimately linked to Jesus and the cross. Jesus' virgin birth, by the miraculous intervention of the Holy Spirit, meant that He did not inherit a sinful human nature like we did. Neither did Jesus commit any sin during His lifetime. Jesus became the only perfect Man, and as such, He was uniquely qualified to put into action God's plan of salvation for mankind. On that cross, Jesus took the punishment of our sin and became our substitute. He suffered the judgment and condemnation of death that our sinful nature and deeds deserve.

5) Faith is essential for salvation. Salvation faith means more than intellectual belief. It involves an act of commitment and trust, in which you commit your life to Jesus Christ and trust Him alone as your Savior and Lord.

"If you confess with your mouth that Jesus is Lord and believe in your heart that God raised Him from the dead, you will be saved." Romans 10:9

Committing your life to Jesus is a personal and individual decision. By praying a prayer like the one on the following page, you are inviting Jesus into your life and choosing to release your every concern to Him.

SALVATION PRAYER

"Jesus, right now, I ask You to become my Savior and the Lord of my life. I believe You died on the cross for my sins, rose from the dead, and are now seated in heavenly places with God, the Father. I believe you have the power and authority to forgive me of all that I have done wrong, and I receive that forgiveness in this moment. No longer desiring to pursue my selfish ways, I completely surrender my life to you. Jesus, I ask You to help me live for You and love others as You love me. Please help me to trust You more each day as I open my heart and life to all that you have prepared before me. Submitting everything within me, I choose to follow You from this day forward. Thank You for Your mercy, hope, and unfailing love. In Your Name I pray, Amen."

If you just prayed to make Jesus your Lord and Savior for the first time or as a recommitment, I hope you will write and tell me about your experience. I would love nothing more than to hear your story and celebrate with you!

CONTACT INFORMATION

To contact Joani for book-related questions, testimonies, or book-signing events, email joani@straighteningmycrown.com

To book Joani for speaking engagements, workshops, or consulting, email joani@joaniwangerin.com

To inquire about photography or event planning, email joani@iconimagine.com

Websites:
joaniwangerin.com
straighteningmycrown.com
iconimagine.com

Join the Movement
Facebook @straighteningmycrown
Instagram @straighteningmycrownnow

ACKNOWLEDGMENTS

A huge thank you to Mary Beth Roosa, Ginny Caligiuri, Laura Coppock, Jane Dozier, and Diann Pajak. You were my final confirmations to sit down and write this book! I hope I made you proud!

Julian Martinez, thank you for offering your incredible gifts to create my logo and design my book cover. You and Meagan have always been ready to support my every artistic endeavor, and there is no one else I would rather have come alongside me on any creative journey.

I could not be more grateful for you Lori McKeating, Bridget Seeley, Ginny Caligiuri, and Jane Dozier and the MANY hours you spent helping me find all of my typos, incomplete sentences, grammatical errors, and... (smile). Beyond your attention to detail, your encouraging words continually inspired me to press on towards my finish line! Thank you so much, ladies!

Thank you, Mark Wangerin, for not only providing my author portraits and the beautiful princess pictures of my granddaughters for this book, but also for introducing me to the world of professional photography. I'm forever grateful for your creative eye, your artistic inspiration, and your generosity in sharing those gifts with me. www.markwangerinphotography.com

Thank you, Mollie Kukkola, for coming to my rescue and formatting my book in the eleventh hour!! I don't know what I would have done without you!

To my three Pastors: Dr. Gary Kinnaman, Dr. Andy Jackson, and Dr. Terry Crist. Thank you for investing in me, believing in me, and pushing me to become who I am today. I am a fruit of your labors!

To Karen DiBernardo, the most inspirational and Godly woman I have ever personally known. Karen challenged me to step into my calling, stood beside me when the trials of life wanted to consume me, fanned the flames of my creativity into flame, and taught me how to enter the Holy of Holies in worship. Thank you, Karen, for your Godly example and inspiring me to trust God with every ounce of my being. I can't wait to see you in heaven, my friend!

To the many whose names are not listed but who are engraved upon my heart. Thank you for your love, support, and friendship!

And ultimately to my Lord and Savior Jesus Christ. You've captured my heart, and it will forever remain Yours...til the end of time and beyond.

ABOUT THE AUTHOR

Born and raised in Texas, Joani's love for the Arts began at the age of 3 when she took her first dance class. Leading roles in school musicals, vocal ensembles, and dance team activities were merely steps to pursuing a degree in dance and theatre education from Stephen F. Austin State University.

Joani moved to Arizona in 1987 where she had a "Damascus Road" encounter with Jesus that radically changed her life. In 1992 Joani joined the staff at Word of Grace Church (a 4000+ member congregation), where she became a licensed and ordained Pastor, directing Creative Service Programming and founding their Theatrical Arts department. Joani also launched a Performing Arts School which eventually supported 200+ students; she produced, directed, wrote and co-wrote multiple stage productions, led hundreds of artistic expressions for weekend worship services, and toured multiple productions internationally.

During her 30 years of ministry, Joani's purview included Weekend Service teams, the Hillsong Ministry School, interns, children and youth ministries for three different campuses. When City of Grace became Hillsong Phoenix, Joani continued her Pastoral duties for two more years utilizing her unique abilities to troubleshoot and build varying departments, while also developing and empowering leaders and volunteer teams.

Joani is a writer, vocalist, photographer, and actress, playing a major role in the movie, "Forevermore: Karla Faye Tucker". Joani is also a gifted teacher and has addressed a wide range of people at conferences, seminars, retreats, weekend services, and schools. She has developed a reputation of spiritual depth and technical quality in artistic expression.

In May of 2017, Joani was diagnosed with breast cancer and that August had a double mastectomy. The next year would encompass not only her battle with cancer, but also her stepping away from her church staff position to launch an Arts School on multiple locations within the Body of Christ.

It is Joani's passionate desire that God would use her creative and leadership gifts, her every trial and hardship, and the many victories she has experienced to encourage the Body of Christ to "Count It All Joy" and realize their potential as God's appointed ambassadors in this world.

Joani has two daughters, one son-in-law, and five grandchildren and she currently resides in Hallsville, Texas.